EXISTO

Worldview and a Meaningful Existence

Neil Soggie

with contributions by
H. Soggie and B. Tysdal

Hamilton Books
A member of
The Rowman & Littlefield Publishing Group
Lanham · Boulder · New York · Toronto · Oxford

Copyright © 2005 by
Hamilton Books
4501 Forbes Boulevard
Suite 200
Lanham, Maryland 20706
Hamilton Books Acquisitions Department (301) 459-3366

PO Box 317
Oxford
OX2 9RU, UK

All rights reserved
Printed in the United States of America
British Library Cataloging in Publication Information Available

Library of Congress Control Number: 2005922491
ISBN 978-0-7618-3167-9

∞™ The paper used in this publication meets the minimum requirements of American National Standard for Information Sciences—Permanence of Paper for Printed Library Materials, ANSI Z39.48—1984

CONTENTS

Preface v
Acknowledgements vii
Introduction: Weltanschauung ix

❧ PART I ~EXISTO: FONS, OPUS, MORTALITAS ❧
*I exist—in the relationship between
my source, my work and my mortality.*

CHAPTER 1   Autopoeics 3
CHAPTER 2   Fons Vitae 13
CHAPTER 3   Opus Vitae 23
CHAPTER 4   Mortalitas 29
CHAPTER 5   Meno's Paradox: Searching for...We Know Not What 35
CHAPTER 6   Religion and Life: The Evidence 39
CHAPTER 7   Experiencing the Tripod: A Guided Imagery Exercise ... 43
CHAPTER 8   Know Thyself: Your Sacred Autobiography 49

❧ PART II ~ MEETING DIFFERENT WORLDVIEWS ❧

Worldview of the New Order: K. Rajaratman 55
Worldview of the Foolish: Erasmus Of Rotterdam 59
Worldview of the Roman Catholic Priest: S. Titus 61
Worldview of the Living Earth: K. Ahenakew 65
Worldview of the Client: E. Spinelli 69
Worldview of the Absolute: C. Shiva Krishna 75
Worldview of the Scientist: Sigmund Freud 81
Worldview of the Unfeeling: Len Eggose 83
Worldview of the Forgiven: The Terrorist 85

Glossary 89
Post-Script: A Theological Reflection 91
References 101
Index of People 133
Index of Topics 135
About the Author and Other Contributors 137

PREFACE

One of the most fundamental drives of every human being is to find meaning in life. We all desire to find a cause, a reason and a passion that will give us energy and make every morning exciting. It is as if we were created to function in a certain way and for a specific purpose, but somehow we cannot seem to get it "quite right" and so we are searching for that "certain WHY" that will make everything fit together in a unified whole.

Certainly our modern, scientific, secularized society tries to give us that "why" with simplistic phrases like, "He who dies with the most toys wins" or "Don't worry...be happy." Yet while we may strive to be happy or successful the issues of chance and the eventual loss experienced in life leave us without a sense of direction. In some, this loss of direction can lead to a deep sense of frustration, emptiness and what certain psychologists call the "existential vacuum" and "noogenic neurosis." In such extreme cases we turn to (whether consciously or unconsciously) self-destructive behaviours and addictions in attempts to fill this existential void.

The purpose of this book is to help you, the reader, to rediscover a sense of meaning, purpose and hope within life. Of course the issue of personal meaning is just that, personal, so in a way I am not qualified to give answers. However, I have discovered that virtually every culture throughout history has come up against this issue of a lack of purpose in life and they have all dealt with it in a relatively predictable way. I hope to share this basic tripod for creating meaning with you so that through your own relationships, beliefs and stories you can find meaning and direction in life. For as Frederick Nietzche states, "The person who lives a **WHY**, can bear almost any **HOW**."

Acknowledgements:

To my mentor, the esteemed and distinguished professor Ernesto Spinelli, I will always be grateful to you for teaching me to suspend the narrative long enough to see another truth.

To my family: Heidi, Jordan and Emily with all my love.

To D.L. Soggie, my father, thank you for showing me the joy of work.

To J.P. Soggie, my mother and my storyteller, the myths will continue on.

Special thanks to Prof. Brian Tysdal for his guidance on this project. Please note that many of the footnote comments intended to balance the author's view are the contribution of this most excellent teacher/ philosopher.

Special thanks also to Larissa Bartos for her editing and preparation of the manuscript.

 A tribute to Maurice Merleau-Ponty
and Soren Kierkegaard.

Introduction

WELTANSCHAUUNG

> *"When we speak of worldviews we mean IDEAS. What is ultimate and total in man, both subjectively, as life-experience and power and character; and objectively, as a world having objective shape."*
>
> ~JASPER

In dealing with the issue of Worldview it is important to understand that it is in essence something that is within the individual, guiding how the individual apprehends and makes sense of the world. Plato, in his allegory of the cave, points out that people of various worldviews often mock each other for their lack of understanding, though those who are mocked may indeed be closer to the objective truth than the mocker.

Often people shy away from discussing or considering their own worldview because it smacks of the dry and irrelevant notions of philosophy. Indeed, it is true that the most noteworthy terminology dealing with worldview, like the German word WELTANSCHAUUNG (meaning Worldview), stem from eighteenth and nineteenth century philosophy. It is important first of all to clarify what a worldview is before we can engage in the more exciting and dynamic process of the "poetry of the self."

Worldview can of course be understood in many ways. Earlier thinkers like Schelling described worldview as an intuitive way of apprehending and interpreting the universe.[1] Many others agree with this basic and natural form of "worldview" (Weltanschauung), where it does not require a theoretical intention and the means of science. For example, Hegel (in his *Phenomenology of the Spirit*) speaks of a "Moral worldview," Gorres uses the term "Poetic worldview" and Ranke speaks of a "Religious or Christian worldview." Schleiermacher says

---

[1] In 1799 (System of Philosophy of Nature) Schelling said that intelligence was productive in two ways: #1. Blindly and unconsciously, or #2. Freely and consciously. That is to say, we unconsciously produce a worldview and consciously produce an ideal world.

that, "It is our worldview that makes our knowledge of God complete." From all of these expressions it is clear that what is generally termed Weltanschauung (worldview) is also part and parcel of our being in the world and indeed grows out of our experiences.

A worldview grows out of inclusive reflection on the world, our being in the world and also our history. Furthermore, while everyone has a worldview, the way this worldview is constructed varies greatly within individuals. For some it is a conscious intent and the result of much existential struggling and theological reflection and study. For others it is an unconscious and emotional way of apprehending the world largely via intuition. We grow up within the process of forming and apprehending a worldview and gradually become accustomed to it. Our worldview is determined by our environment, our race, socio-economic status, culture and our health and relationships and indeed emerges as a part of being in the world. For most people a worldview is not an issue of theoretical knowledge, but is retained in one's memory as a coherent conviction that guides our current affairs. It is in a way our orientation and sense of self along with a mixture of superstition and knowledge and prejudice and sober reason.

It can be argued that a worldview in a personal sense, then, is different than the formal discipline of philosophy. In a proper sense, Kant would say that Philosophy is the conscious control and skill of reason to draw meaning from concept and to establish systematic interconnections between ideas. However, as Prof. Brian Tysdal points out below, Kant also held that one's "reality" is a combination of environmental data (empiricism) and mental awareness (rationalism):

> The data from one's environment is filtered through established mental "categories" that order the data. In a sense, one's mind "creates" one's reality. One needs an outside environment in order for there to be "data," but this is not sufficient in itself to create "meaning." Mind is not sufficient in and of itself to create meaning either simply because there is not implicit in the mind the necessary environmental data. Kant would say you "experience" absolutely nothing without the combined elements of data and mind. It would seem a paralyzing paradox of needing both in order to "start" the process of awareness. This would cause me then to see one's "self" as a process of simultaneous emergence. [Hence in many ways there is little difference] between the pristine "story" of worldview creation and the attempts of philosophy to describe the same thing.

It is clear that the notion of worldview is not so much an objective notion as it is a personal experience and way of forming "who we are." Therefore, the study of worldview is not irrelevant and dry. Indeed it is one of the most personal and dynamic and poetic of experiences, for in a way it guides and frames how we will apprehend and engage the world wherein we live. In essence then, worldview is the material of life itself and the skeleton whereupon personal meaning is layered.

I.

Chapter One

AUTOPOEICS[2]

"Humans do not only have consciousness, which is what makes the synthesis of incongruous elements possible. They also possess self-consciousness, which means that the synthesis is not a static, completed object, but a dynamic process. Furthermore, the process is one I have some hand in shaping. The power of self-consciousness means that I am always in some sense "outside myself." Or, to be more exact, I am a never-finished process of relating myself to self. There is the self that I have become, and there is the self that I project myself as becoming. I am in the process of moving from one to the other."
~EVANS, 1990

Often scholars speak of Weltanschauung as something personal that allows us to form meaning from the world around us. When we discuss the topic of personal meaning we may think that we can all agree as to what this topic means. However for the sake of clarity I consider it important to first evaluate the basic principle of "I" and "thou" and the nature of personal identity. Once we have a fairly clear appreciation of this overwhelmingly complex process of what is "personal" we can then explore the phenomenon known as "meaning." Only then will we begin to be able to grasp the fundamental intricacies of Weltanschauung.

In many ways the notion of our "self" as static and consistent is utterly false. We must therefore begin by developing a clear understanding of our own bodily essence. Once this basic issue is clarified we can then move on to the nature of our existence and the meaning or meanings to be found therein. As we progress through this exploration we will undoubtedly discover that the journey is much more complex and fluid than we ever conceived possible.

We can consider ourselves firstly to be human beings. We are living creatures that are made up of billions of cells that are organized in different ways to provide different functions. However, we are not only ourselves, as billions of cells, we are also integrated into the environment, for if the

---

[2] Literally meaning the "Creating of the Self."

environment is not supportive of the cellular requirements we cease to exist in our essence as bodily human beings.

So we must also begin with the obvious issues of bodily essence that correspond with ecological issues. We cannot consider ourselves individuals in utter isolation for we are integrally connected with a myriad of systems within this world that support and sustain our bodily essence. In that sense we are part of the earth and must always remember that there is not a great distinction molecularly between humus (dirt) and humanity. Indeed, it is important to remember the old West-Semitic creation narrative that declares that humanity was formed out of the dust and the breath of life was placed therein.

At this point we will take a look at "what we are" through the reductionistic perspective: namely we are a community of cells.

In this there is of course the dependence of the cells upon the environment for both materials and energy. The two issues we encounter from a phenomenological observation in science are that "life comes from life" and "life is information." To this we acknowledge that the organizing information of life is DNA and the more fundamental base sequences that form it. Yet, DNA alone is useless and cannot facilitate the formation of environmental materials and energy. There must also be the once organized system of materials and energy that is guided by the DNA in order for further life to be produced. Therefore we must acknowledge that life COMES from life (though we will continue to struggle with issues of origins for millennia to come) and that life is also information that guides the continuation of this existing dynamic system.

So what makes us different from our environment? It is clear that a boundary is necessary for the essence of life to form. A boundary is in place that separates us from the environment. On the cellular level this is done through a semi-permeable membrane that is flexible enough to allow for growth and changes in the ecological context of the cell, yet strong enough to not allow a diffusion of the inner portions of the cell. The boundary of the cell therefore establishes an environment for the systems of life to engage in their DNA guided process of metabolism and reacting/interacting with the external environment.

Each cell is endowed with its own cognition skills. No matter the type of cell, the outer boundary follows a set of rules that interact with the environment. The cellular walls will react to certain compounds by becoming an almost impenetrable barrier, while on the other hand, if these compounds are required by the internal metabolism of the cell, it will open ion gates to absorb the needed nutrients. While some may argue whether or not this is actual "thinking" it is undeniably a system supporting interactive function that comes very close to cellular thinking.[3]

Once cellular identity is affirmed by means of a barrier, the next step is to ascertain the nature of the cell and how it functions within its environment. This of course is important not only for the cell, as it will determine whether it remains in an ecological state that supports its own functioning, but also how it functions within the larger system.

Finally, there is the observed biological prime directive of "perpetuation of life," or reproduction, for life comes from life and this means a balanced perpetuation on both the micro and macro level. For example, in higher order organisms such as human beings each cell has the biological impetus to reproduce and replace the dying and decaying. However, uncontrolled reproduction on the micro level can have drastic consequences on the macro level, for uncontrolled reproduction of cellular bodies within a larger life system is in essence cancerous and will disrupt the overall functioning of that life system. Once that larger environmental life system is thrown into sufficient disequilibrium then the death of the entire environment (or higher organism) occurs and thus also the death of the variety of cellular life that makes up that system.[4]

So it is important that cellular life at its basic form be able to "manage itself within its environmental system." Only in so doing can the rates of micro level reproduction meet the drive of the cell to reproduce, and still support the macro-level requirements of maintaining a positive environment for the cell and its descendents. In a sense, then, each cell must fulfill its meaning within the larger system, otherwise the future of its progeny is in jeopardy.

---

[3] Prof. Brian Tysdal notes that Plato long ago stated that a human being, in essence, is nothing but soul; the physical has nothing to offer but negative influence on the rational soul. Prof. Tysdal notes that *"This gnostic hyperspirituality of Plato and Augustine has had a negative effect on Christian anthropology and our culture's understanding of the self* (look for his forthcoming book on this subject). *What is of special value here is the fact that what is often attributed only to one "part" of the human person (e.g. souls think, bodies sense physically), is may be not so cut and dried. The human person is only that—a human—when considered as a whole. The whole interacts (like the community of persons within oneself) and is expressed when we see the body sweating when one feels anxious, or conversely (and mostly ignored) when one cannot think clearly when one has not had enough sleep. WE ARE WHOLE BEINGS."*

[4] An interesting side note is that the *Revelation of St. John* describes this type of disequilibrium on the macro/global environmental level.

In this process we see the basics of two distinctive processes essential to meaning making. The first, autopoeics[5], is the process of defining one's self apart from the environment (literally "making the self"). This can of course be best understood as the cell relating with and engaging with the environment in order to create within itself an environment that is somehow qualitatively different from the diffused environment outside the cell. As Capra (2000) notes, the two essentials of this process at the cellular level are the physical boundary of the cell wall, and the function of the metabolic network within that cellular wall. The second process then is how that individual (whether that be a cell or higher organism) fits into the functioning and maintaining of the larger environment. This is known as the mythopoeic process (literally "making the story") because it is the dynamic story of interacting with the environment and fulfilling the role of the self within that environment.

We may learn from the cellular level that these basic processes are essential not only to understanding ourselves, but also to defining ourselves and the meaning that we create and experience within this dynamic process called life. However, we must be clear that the "defining" process is dynamic and *only* found in relationship with others, ourselves and the environment. Personal meaning cannot be found unless we relate with others in some way, thereby dynamically framing the direction of our self-defining process (and this is both partially deterministic and self-guided). Secondly, meaning cannot be made unless we have located that defined self within a larger environmental context of not only time and space, but function as well.[6]

---

[5] The terms mythopoeics and autopoeics are defined in the **terms** section in the back of the book.

[6] I wish to highlight here some observations of Prof. Brian Tysdal because he has done a far better job than I in attempting to express what I have set out in the previous paragraph: *"Martin Buber holds that no "I" exists apart from a "You." He states that the only true expression of "I" is found in encountering "wholes." These wholes are borderless "others" that not only give me frame of reference to understand myself but also to become more aware of who the other is as well. When I give up the control of trying to define the other, I then am open to encountering the borderless whole. It would seem that I have little control over both my borderless self and the borderless realities of those I encounter (other people, God, nature). Choice exists in my functioning in a world where sin has dichotomized whole people, and the choices I make are probably first conditioned to some degree, but more importantly result in exerting control over my environment which then establishes limiting borders on self. I'm not sure that our effort to define ourselves is even the right question to be asking: If there is no "I" without a "You" then it would seem that my concern would be more to do with encountering the others that are borderless and beyond definition. In fact, all whole people defy "definition." Not sure exactly where this leads because I do not deny*

So what are we? We are communities of cells that work in an open system toward a common goal of existence. In essence we as human beings are not simply one entity with a boundary between the self and environment (i.e. skin). We are an open and dynamic system of communities of cells working and relating WITH the environment that produces one seamless united experience known as "personhood."

Therefore, using the words of the reductionist, we are a cellular network that is materially and energetically open, with a constant flow of energy and molecules that produces a relative equilibrium within the cells and within the larger community of cells. So in a sense, we, in our bodily essence, are the summative experience of relationships between specialized communities of cells, all working for a common purpose, our "personhood".

For some, of course, this level of reductionism is too abstract to make much sense. So let us now consider the realm of the mind. While considering ourselves a summative experience in the cellular sense may seem strange, when we explore the nature and function of the mind we discover how true this summative role is in what it means to be human and an individual.

Within our brains are various communities of cells that actually constitute the many "people" that we are as individuals. There is, for example, the visual sense that picks up light and transmits the neural energy via rods and cones through towards the back of the brain to the occipital lobe where it is diffused, interpreted and processed, and at that point we experience the sense of sight. Yet this information must then be disseminated to other parts of the brain via the thalamus in order to make meaning out of this sense, transforming the act from sensing to perceiving.

So what are the different communities of cells within the brain and how do they help dictate and define our bodily essence as human beings? Within each of us there are powerful drives toward pleasure, aggression, power and wild emotions. This base section of the brain, encompassing the brain stem and limbic system, is that secret part of us that longs for the pleasures of this world. It is at times a part of us that we may wish did not exist in our "civilized" world, yet in the end we could not live or survive or even breath without this community of cells.

Next to this base community of cells resting below the occipital lobe is a small ball-shaped community of cells that looks as if it is a small separate brain, and indeed that it what it is called, the Cerebellum (meaning "small brain"). This community of cells is a massive storehouse of unconscious memories of conditioning and information about basics of functioning like how to walk, tie

---

that we make choices, but I do wonder if these choices are the essential bedrock of our existential self."

our shoes, etc. Every time we do our everyday activities we are communicating and acting largely under the practical guidance of the cerebellum.

Our conscious sensations as well as decision making for movement are in the parietal lobe resting upon the top of the brain. Here we decide to move a finger or toe and then the information is transmitted through the thalamus, along with guiding information from the cerebellum, to the appropriate limb. This concert or harmony of persons within us is how we are able to survive and move within our bodily selves.

Next are our silent and vocal selves. Our silent person is located in the right temporal lobe and is the temporal coordinating person within us. It is the one that thinks quietly about the past and indeed is able to place itself within the past or the future. It is the "time-traveller" that helps to locate us in our context and incorporates ancient myths and our own personal history into the intricate tapestry of our personal story. We experience this person most often when we have those quiet moments to daydream. This person is one who is hidden and only finds external expression when his partner, the left temporal lobe, listens to and agrees with what the right temporal lobe is saying.

The left temporal lobe is the language self—the part that remembers the various languages from music to mathematics, to Shakespeare—and this person is the spokesperson for all of the other persons within you. At times this person may seem to be a weakling while at others this person may be a wild autonomous ruler. How others view you is likely constructed from the person expressed by your left temporal lobe.

Our symbolic, theoretical, philosophical, problem-solving self is in the front of the brain. This is the person that cannot stand to live with meaninglessness and will draw on all the resources of the other persons to resolve issues. If for example I were to say, "Imagine a nose coming out of a fire in a fireplace" immediately that frontal lobe person would pull the meaning of the words "nose," "fire" and "fireplace" from the left temporal lobe. Then it would pull the images of these things stored within the occipital lobe, and finally draw upon past memories involving these three issues allowing them to form in the right temporal lobe. Immediately the frontal lobe will have constructed a story to fill out the meaninglessness of this image. Suddenly you find your frontal lobe and right temporal lobes working together to create an experience for you that brings you back to a time when you sat by a Christmas fireplace, imagining Santa Claus dropping down and getting caught in the fire and then quickly rushing out of the flames to avoid being burnt. This seamless interaction is not only a testament to the level of cooperation within you, but to the power of stories to create a seamless experience of meaning.

Finally, the last person is found within the pre-frontal lobe, as it remembers the guiding principles that others have taught you. The rules, guidelines, principles and basic precepts that this person holds are what you experience as your principles. This is your conscience, and it is well connected with the other portions of the brain, particularly the brain stem, ready to flood you with negative emotions if you stray too far from its expectations.

As you can see, each one of these persons is you. Yet none of them are you alone, and none can give even the qualitative experience of "being you" except in relation to all the other persons within you. If you lose one part you will not cease being you, though it may appear that way to others. For example if you have a stroke in the right temporal lobe you may lose much of your own secret personal memories and most cherished dreams, but to others it will seem as though little if nothing happened because you can still talk and function normally. However, if that same little stroke were to occur not to the silent part of you, but to the vocal left temporal lobe (*Broca* or *Wernicke* regions) then people would consider it an utter tragedy. You would in some ways be viewed as a vegetable as in one fell swoop you lost your ability to communicate with others.

This is indeed still only part of the picture, for we are also a product of our embodied experiences. It is clear that these communities of cells are connected with the larger experience of embodiment and as such are expressed in our bodily essence while reflecting our historical existence. Romanyshyn gives an excellent example of this. A woman is walking down the street, but whenever a man walks by her, she unreflectively pulls her coat across her breasts in order to hide her breasts. She is not consciously or reflectively aware of doing this, but for a community of cells in our mind, at the embodied, lived level of engagement, this is an intentional, meaningful act, even if pre-reflective. Now, suppose someone notices this and calls it to her attention. She may then, perhaps even with surprise, note that she was not aware of this act. Yet if she explored this, she would likely discover that this pre-reflective act is meaningful and has a history. One can imagine that the woman sees men as sexual predators who objectify her body and are a threat. Hence the silent mind/cerebellum-based act of covering her breasts is an act that disallows her breasts to be objectified by the gaze of those men.

If we explored further with this woman, we may find that she had a negative sexualized experience in which a man had stared at her breasts prior to being aggressive toward her. All of this history is contained in that lived, embodied, pre-reflective act of covering her breasts, and conscious or not, is part of who she is and her embodied meaning as she walks down the street.

Philosophers like Sartre, Husserl or Merleau-Ponty might say that our history becomes "sedimented" in our bodily gestures, contained there as latent and un-reflected upon even though it is meaningful and lived out in the world. Psychoanalysts like Freud may then contend that to make these meanings thematic and subject to reflection is the process of making the unconscious, conscious, or making the pre-thematic, thematic, in a sense following the ancient Greek call to "know thyself."

One can of course see that there is a kind of freedom in this: in freeing her lived, pre-reflective experience to the level of thematic reflection, what had previously been lived unknowingly can then be subject to a choice. The woman may choose to no longer fear men, to move beyond the embodied meaning of her past, and to cease her previously latent act of covering her breasts, if she wishes to do so.

Who are we? We are the relationships between the various levels of embodied experiences. We are a seamless and summative experience of communities of cells. We are dependent upon these cells for our existence and our functioning. We as individuals are the comprehensive organism that is therefore responsible for the amassed experiences and decisions. Yet in the end we are not one, but many, as we are a complex system that must seek to work in balance and harmony, not only within itself, but also with the environment upon which we depend for our bodily essence.

So it is clear that what is "personal" is very much a community experience (we only know ourselves in relationship with others), not just socially, but even within ourselves, as we learn to communicate to ourselves within ourselves. In working through this "personal" communication we come to the issue of meaning. As we experience our total self, we are struck with the question of purpose and how we as summative relational creatures fit into the larger environment. In this way, then, we need to develop a comprehensive story that helps us to fill in the gaps of information (because we simply do not know enough). This summative story is then where we shift from our autopoeics to mythopoeics (*mythos* = story; *poein* = creating). We are no longer defining ourselves, but creating a larger story within which we can be located (our *Weltanschuung*). Obviously then the two processes are interdependent as the self-creating process (autopoeics) and the story-creating process (mythopoeics) are never static but constantly redefining the other.[7]

Meaning then is an emergent phenomenon of process placing the individual in a mythopoeic context allowing autopoeic functioning. Meaning then resides neither in the individual nor in myths about past or future or in community.

---

[7] It is this process that is traditionally known as *Existence* and is the domain of the philosophical discipline of existentialism. So it is clear that we as people cannot be defined in an "essence" since we are relationships and must be defined by, in and through our existence (which then forms our essence ... hence Sartre's famous phrase, "Existence precedes essence").

Meaning is however an emergent subjective phenomena of the coordinating summative experience.[8]

In looking at the history of the world and considering the long history of human mythopoeics (specifically faith stories) it is clear that there are three basic structures required for finding personal meaning: **a source, a work** and a way to find hope even in the face of **death**. We will take the remainder of this book to explore the tripod of structures (see fig. 1) people use to draw meaning from their existence: **Fons; Opus; Mortalitas**, finding a meaningful existence (and understanding our own worldview) in the interrelationship between our source, our work and the limits of our mortal experience.

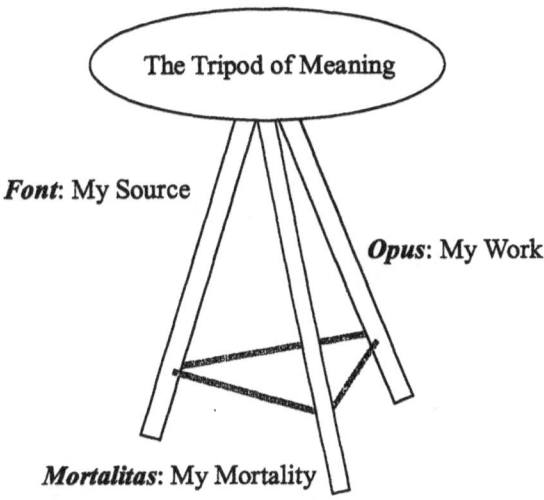

Figure 1. The Tripod of Meaning

---

[8] Prof. Brian Tysdal offers a balance to the autopoeics—"making the self" process. He warns that we must not be deceived by believing we have more control than we do over the overall process of forming the self and that we are not solely (or nearly so) responsible for choosing the elements of my "I." One "defines" oneself; one "makes" oneself; etc. fundamentally by the "choosing" that brings meaning. This does not necessarily mean that it is entirely "self" affirming. Prof. Tysdal would say that our *"Identity building has very much to do with outside influences simply acting upon me with little to no regard for my choices. I have been accused of "soft" determinism but I think a middle ground between autonomous choice and harsh determinism is needed."*

Chapter Two

FONS VITAE

> *"A person is a historical being. An individual is not born in the world of things, persons and time as a finished product. The being is not prior to history. The person becomes what they are through the history of relations of environment and relations of self. The individual is not therefore, simply a being in the world, but comes into being with the world."*
> ~RUBEM ALVES

One of the ultimate questions that frames our worldview is the question of origin. What is the source of our being and how does this inform our role or purpose in life? Whether it is religion, philosophy or science, the basic issue of the nature of the font from which we spring is essential and central to our self-understanding. Here again we see the intricate interplay of mythopoeics[9] influencing our autopoeic process.

When dealing with the issue of origins we are not interested in seeking the objective "truth" at this point. Rather we will simply explore the facets of this epistemological issue that is so essential to our own personal meaning making process. For what we view ourselves as springing forth from will determine not only our actions and responsibilities in life, but also dictate how we approach the issues of personal suffering and death.

In a very basic way, then, our existential font (what we view as the source of our existence) is central to our understanding of life (*fons vitae* then literally means "life's source"), for in essence life and its significance are defined only by relationships to other things. Without relationships life itself is meaningless, as we will not have a reference from which to communicate with ourselves or define ourselves. Therefore, with this in mind we will explore the various mythic structures for understanding our source, beginning with the great modern interpretive story developed by Charles Darwin.

"The Origins of Species," published in 1859, popularized the notion that all existing organisms emerged from less complex life in the distant past; that

---

[9] The terms mythopoeics and autopoeics are defined in the **terms** section in the back of the book.

through the principle of mutations organisms came to better "fit" the environment and therefore live. In essence the idea takes advantage of the uncertainty left in the transmission of genes from one generation to another. In this way the environment influences and selects the primary genes for the species and therefore, given enough time, Darwin theorized that higher organisms could have emerged.

However, this does bring up an interesting issue that is central in much of the debate about the need for a Neo-Darwinian ecological approach to evolution and the origin of life. The concepts put forward by Darwin ignore the basic fact that life is not one "thing" but a summative experience of an open and dynamic system of interplay between various organisms and a supportive environment. Without one, the other cannot exist.

The notion of molecular evolution took hold in the second quarter of the twentieth century. This idea arose in recognition of the integrated nature of life as well as serious problems with Darwinian evolution. Molecular evolution posits that molecules randomly formed the requisite compounds required to support life and that they further developed in molecular complexity resulting in cycles with self-reinforcing feedback loops.

In this construct, often called Pre-biotic Evolution because it is evolution occurring before the formation of basic life, there was an evolution of inanimate matter. In one version of this theory these complex compounds eventually formed a primitive enzyme and, as some RNA also function as enzymes, this primitive enzyme acted as RNA and a catalyst for primitive metabolism. Through this eventual process of metabolic action, life emerged. When these primitive cellular actions found themselves in a self-reinforcing molecular cycle the evolution of life was able to proceed.

No matter what one thinks of either of these basic origin theories, what is inherent to them both is the lack of a purpose. Why is this important? A purpose is simply the last goal of a series of sequential goals. Ultimately, a "meaning" is a rational explanation for the choice of one's purpose in life. In essence, a purpose in life gives meaning to all goals that help in its achievement. If, however, our guiding stories tell us that we have arisen from a purposeless nothing and toward a cosmic series of accidents, there is no ultimate purpose.

Therefore, in the end, both of these spontaneous generation ideas of life from non-life come to the inevitable conclusion of cyclical meaninglessness. As the ancients have said, "Meaningless, meaningless, all is meaningless. The sun rises and the sun sets and there is nothing new under the sun." This ultimate problem of drawing meaning of existence from a font of spontaneous generation is made clear in the pointlessness of the Darwinian construct of reality:

> Meaninglessness is essentially endless pointlessness, and meaningfulness is therefore the opposite. Activity, and even long, drawn out and repetitive

activity, has a meaning if it has some significant culmination, some more or less lasting end that can be considered to have been the direction and purpose of the activity...(However) this life of the world thus presents itself to our eyes as a vast machine, feeding on itself, running on and on forever to nothing... then one realizes that there is no point at all, that it really culminates to nothing, that each of these cycles, so filled with toil, is to be followed only by more of the same.

~TAYLOR, 1981

This problem of meaninglessness resulting from a scientific answer to the issue of *origins* is due to the very nature of the scientific method. In essence the proper use of the scientific method is to allow gaps in knowledge to exist and to continue to struggle to fill those gaps, not with myths but with testable facts. So there is a very natural tension between proper science and Darwinian scientific mythopoeics.

This more modern issue brings to mind the ancient call of the educational reformer Erasmus of Rotterdam in the early 1500's. Educating and working in the backdrop of a rigid Vatican dogmatic, Erasmus encouraged his students to question the dominant mythic structures of the day by going back and first evaluating the source of these stories. From this line of education, the famous phrase of Erasumus changed the intellectual world and spurred on the greatest upheaval in Christendom. "AD FONTIS" (that famous Erasmus phrase) means simply, "Go back to the sources." In the case of the disciples of Erasmus this meant railing against the rigid mythic/theological structure for salvation set out by a corrupt Pope, and going back to the Christian scriptures (the accepted source for information about salvation) to see if this source did indeed mandate the rigid mythic/theological structure dictated by the Vatican. In some cases like with Martin Luther and John Calvin (and of course many other 16th century C.E. reformers), the conclusion was that the source demanded that the existing theological structure be changed and refined.

When trying to understand our own human experience we, too, need to go back to the sources (whatever they may be). Some may argue that a good neo-Darwinian theory can do this. However in the end there are three issues that must be dealt with on the very human level. The first one is that science in its proper experimental sense cannot answer questions of origins because these are beyond the phenomenological nature of the scientific method. Secondly, we must be mindful that any philosophy (scientific or not) cannot answer all the questions that a dynamic human life demands (because life is simply too complex and dynamic for even the most advanced of philosophies). Thirdly is the important nature of people and the fact that they are formed in relationships.

This issue of the relational nature of humanity supercedes the question about whether our source can be answered in a philosophical or scientific sense.

Therefore the problem of origin is transformed from "answering" the question to, "Is there a **relationship** where these questions may be placed?" For in the end human beings require relationships, above all else, in order to frame and organize their own existence. In the end, then, we need a "religion" and not a "philosophy" or "scientific explanation" of origin as the first leg of the tripod of meaning. For only in a religion is the "I – Thou" relationship found, where issues of ultimate source can be set up relationally as a way of ordering one's worldview. Only in this religious/mythopoeic relationship then is that source and guiding mythic narrative formed. It is in reality a relationally based and dynamic font myth that frames "where questions may be placed" rather than answering all the ultimate questions of source, for such a task is beyond the scope of philosophy or science proper.

Many, of course, rail against the notion of "needing" a religion or a relationship with a transpersonal being/creator. In an age of technology it is natural to want to live based only upon our reason, knowledge and scientific pursuits, but in the end, however, this is not enough. Why? Simply because, even though we want to believe that we "know enough," actual knowledge proves to be fragmentary and we quickly come to the realization that we know very little.

We must recognize within this that there are three levels of knowledge that are dealt with within the human experience. As Emmanuel Kant clarified, the highest level of knowledge is the **Noumena**—reality as it really exists in all its depths of complexity. This means not just its observable qualities but its sub-molecular qualities, even to the level of the mysterious dark matter and beyond. **Knowledge of the noumena is what we strive for, but will never fully know.**

The next level of knowledge is the level of the **phenomenon**. The phenomenon is that which we can observe and experience (sometimes by aid of technology) ... not a full explanation of reality but it is a small part of it. Our knowledge, particularly our scientific knowledge, is, in its proper sense, phenomenological, and therefore what we really know is fragmentary and incomplete. **Phenomenon is what we observe.**

However, it is within the third level of knowledge that human beings truly live (whether we want to admit it or not). This is the **mythic** level. The **mythic level** is how this relates to me. It is the story or explanation of how a phenomenon relates to "me" as an embodied individual, and whether we like it or not, this is where knowledge always leads back to. The reality is that in virtually every culture in history this mythic level is framed in a specific manner—"Religion" and "Belief".

Let us take a moment to consider the limitations of our own knowledge. For example, do you know what a radio is? In other words, could you make a radio "from scratch?" Generally what we know is only a self made story of how something relates to us. Do you know what paper is? "Of course...it is the white sheets in this book that I am reading." (Hence most of what we know is in terms of relationships.) Even scientific knowledge always leads back to the mythic level of "how it relates to me" because otherwise our utter ignorance of the reality of life would be overwhelming. The same is true with virtually every pursuit of knowledge—eventually we run up against a wall and are left with only two things, a relationship and a mystery. Let me quote an unnamed colleague/astronomer:

> As scientists we have answered the questions of diseases and created technology beyond belief. We have peered into the distant past of the universe and have learned the secrets to unleash the very power that holds the universe together. We have even gone back to discover the birth of stars, galaxies, and even to the first second of the existence of the universe. Yet, for all of our achievement, when we climb the highest peak...and reach the pinnacle of scientific achievement...as we climb onto that summit...we find sitting there a group of theologians that have been sitting there for centuries.

In essence what my colleague is saying is we can go only so far with science. There will ALWAYS be more questions and more mysteries—we will always have to go further (it is the very nature of scientific pursuit). There will always be another wall that needs to be peered around, there will always be the unknowable, and we will always need a construct of "god" as a place to relegate these mysteries to. No matter what scientific explanation we may have for our "source" we will therefore always need God in order for it to be meaningful. Meaning is a summative experience that is only found in the working out of relationships between the self, others, the environment and the transpersonal.

This is of course not surprising to those who study the nature of meaning within the human psyche. For (as Kierkegaard pointed out) the importance of religion has always been recognized as an essential part of the existential makeup of a person. So too, the mythopoeics of origin must have some role of a god within it. In line with this inevitable direction of the search for meaning, we are constantly reminded of the nature of framing meaning from one's existential font. For it appears that it is not so much the answer of the questions that are important, but rather simply having a relationship or "place" from which we spring, and a relationship within which to put the mysteries of our source. So, in making meaning in our existence, especially of loss, suffering and death (the popular domain of the existential philosopher) it is not necessarily ANSWERING THE QUESTIONS, but having a place/relationship wherein to PUT THE QUESTIONS. It appears that this source relationship is ultimately important to satisfying our sense of meaninglessness. That is, it appears that the mere fact of being able to put these mysteries at the feet of God is powerful in our human functioning and ability to organize our worldview.

Therefore, it is clear that a creation myth is important for organizing a worldview and creating meaning within life. These creation stories are common in virtually every culture and at virtually every age. They contain within them the basic conception of the natural or initial order of things and articulate the beginning of the people. There is also central to all of these stories a relationship to a creator, as well as a basic statement about that people's relationship with nature. It is within these relationships that people have rooted themselves and sprung forth to create meaning in their work and in the intangible struggles of life.

An example of this web of relationships within a creation myth is the story told by the aboriginal peoples of the American southern plains. In their story the creator made the world and began to cover it with water. The first and only man who was made by the creator stood on a piece of dry land and ran to the waters, telling them where to stop. After this was done, this first man, called Lone Man, spent his time trying to figure out where he came from (he was struggling with his existential foundation and story of origin). Then the creator arrived, walking upon the water, and the two of them discussed where they came from.

In the course of their discussions and wanderings the two worked together to create the land, the animals, and plants upon the land. Then finally the creator left Lone Man alone, and a buffalo helped teach Lone Man how to live in this new land. So, then, all the descendents of Lone Man from generation to generation were to conduct ceremonies to remember who they were. At these ceremonies Lone Man decreed that a buffalo skull be present, to honour the buffalo that helped Lone Man learn how to live in the land and plant and dry tobacco.

Within this story there is clearly a connection with the creator and a series of significant relationships that help "locate" the people and organize their cosmological world. This creation myth serves to illustrate that myths about relationships—to an unseen creator, and to the tangible physical world—are more powerful than a scientific attempt to explain origins in some technical terms. What people are longing for, and seem to require as an organizing force in their lives, is a relationship to the source and a story that frames that relationship, not a comprehensive explanation of existence. Again, it appears that "answering the question of source" is not as important as a "relationship" or a "place to put questions about one's source or origin."

This of course is a central human need, and even the scientific community cannot help but engage in the mythopoeics of our source. One example of this is a statement given at the Nobel Conference in 1997, *"All the molecules in your body were formed inside stars. We are the future of ancient stars."* In a way then, whether it is religion or science, or even science fiction, the basic story of how we relate to the universe is where we begin to draw meaning:

> Then I will tell you a great secret, Captain, perhaps the greatest of all time. The molecules of your body are the same molecules that make up this station, and the nebula outside—that burn inside the stars themselves. We are star-stuff. We are the Universe made manifest, trying to figure itself out.
> ~DELENN, BABYLON 5 (science fiction television series)

In the case of the three great religions of Judaism, Christianity and Islam there is the great font story of Adam and Eve. In this story creation marks the beginning, and God is defined in a unique nature of the self, relating to the self, within the self, but still with a full unity of purpose and action. In its simplistic narrative that presents itself in the form of an ancient myth, even the scientific issues of life existence are explained, for in the literal creation narrative a picture of a full and comprehensive system of "in-systems" creation is presented. That is, all the systems required for supporting life are all created in full functioning form by the act of the creator. Surprisingly, such a model (scientifically) is required for life, as we presently know it, to exist.

Then humanity is made, with a myriad of meaningful relationships already set forth. First, the human being is made in the image of God. Whatever this may mean, it does connote a deep level of intimacy and relationship (almost kinship) between humanity and the great and apparently all-powerful creator. Through the very relational nature of humans then this relationship provides us with an object for our identification bonds; a first parent, if you will, that we are to model. From this relationship we learn who we are and how we are to organize ourselves, both within ourselves and with others.

Secondly is the formation of the relationship between the sexes. The initial picture is the unity of purpose between the sexes and the equality of the sexes. This is done in a duality of the term "helper," for while the term given to the woman is "helper" and while the term may suggest subjugation of this sex, the term is later applied to the creator, utterly erasing any hint of subjugation. Therefore, both sexes are to be engaged in a purpose, a unity of purpose, almost as the divine creator is a fullness of being relating to itself and within itself, yet with a unity of purpose.

Thirdly is the source story that gives wings to the form of the *Opus* of humanity. That is, the human was created in relationship with the creator and in relationship with the creation. As the image of the creator, the human was then to also be the image in function, as caretaker of creation. Implicit in this then is that we are created to care for and nurture creation as well as designed to be an integral part of creation. This of course rails against the notion of some religious movements that call for a separation of the physical and the psychic/ spiritual.

Finally, in the midst of this font story is a warning/ prediction of what is commonly known as "the fall." The original humans disobey the creator, resulting in the entrance of suffering and death into the realm of the human experience along with the failure on the part of humanity to fulfill its proper role as caretaker. Yet, even implicit within this declaration/prediction is a promise of the creator ultimately repairing creation and saving humanity (and all of creation in the charge of humanity) from the inevitable end of utter annihilation. In the midst of all of this are the base guiding relationship and the full frame of relationships that guide and form the existential source of humanity.

Of course, the full and adequate source myths that define the essential relationships will facilitate our autopoeic process. This of course means that the nexus necessary for a meaningful existence is not limited to transpersonal religious myths. There are also the essential and more personal relationships that form each individual's own personal myths and define the uniqueness of each person in identity; that is, the ancestral, cultural and familial stories that also form the unique identity of the self.

The font (that first leg of the tripod of meaning and worldview) is of course then also one's "family of origin" story. It is of course the full spectrum of stories, how our ancestors defined themselves in their work and their own inevitable mortality, that also helps to form our source from which we spring (thereby giving a sense of direction to our lives). This of course is more in the realm of psychology than religion, but again forms part of that first essential leg of the tripod of meaning.

Even as adults we must continually revisit and redefine our own source/childhood experiences and the meanings they create within us. We must not allow the child within us to limit the growth of our existence, but simply recognize it as a part of the process of forming who we are. It is important to remember that we are historical beings, continually moving from what we were towards what we project ourselves to be becoming. We are a never-ending interaction of relationships and myths that are dynamic and always summative in their ever-present experience.

In such a way then our existence is partially a linear progression of past, present and future. Yet because we can continually and temporally project ourselves into our past, revisit, and in some fashion "reconstruct" our memories, it is also cyclical and non-linear. Indeed, depending upon what "person"/brain structure we are listening to, our conscious experience of the present may be of a sensation laden present, a memory filled past or a hope-filled future. So it may be said that we are a cyclical eruption of our past into our future.

This dynamic imagery of "erupting" through the present then provides the aura that we exist in a dynamic and fluid experience where our existence is inextricably connected to past, present and future. Hence whilst the precedent does not cause the present (in a rigid linear deterministic sense), it does instigate our current encounter with the world (and thereby influences our dynamic worldview). It is the prism that shades and organizes how we greet the emerging circumstances of life. In taking up our source story, we do not simply apply it to the present, but use it to act within our present. In a sense, then, our personal existence continually emerges into the present, but always takes on the reflection and colour of the past (a simple illustration of this is the fact that your past allows you to understand the lines on this page in its thoughts/words).

Our very being then, and how we understand, construct and make sense of our being, is therefore formed as we move towards the future. The "fountain from which we spring," therefore, is a very apt image. The water springs forth from the ground, constantly pushing us forward. We may choose to fight against the flow, but we will never succeed. Rather, the way to make life easier is to live in the direction that the water is flowing, projecting ourselves into the future with our plans giving an orientation to life and helping us feel like we are engaging in the flow of life, rather than simply being swept along by it.

Living, existing and springing forth from a "source" "history" or "font" is therefore inescapable if we are to have a direction and meaning in life. We all have a past and our past shapes and forms our experiences. What is essential is to understand, discover and in a sense, "create" a clear understanding of our past. In so doing we may better orient ourselves within the ever-flowing stream of life and set a course that takes us towards an acceptable end point. It is also important to remember that each moment we are a new person, fleeting and dynamic and in the process of becoming as we live within the world relating to the world, to ourselves, and to our God.

Chapter Three

OPUS VITAE

> *"Living means negotiating conflict, facing contradiction, tolerating paradox—we are always somewhere in between: no more and not yet, between birth and death, freedom and necessity, isolation and belonging, faith and doubt. Embracing life means daring to greet the inevitable suffering, anxiety and guilt as an intrinsic part of existence and as an opening up of our own horizons and possibilities."*
> ~VAN DEURZEN, 2001

The next step in our discussion of Weltanschauung is to explore how our worldview both forms and is formed by our actions. That is, how does being in the world and activity within the world interact with our existence and its meaning? This issue of the existential *Opus*, making meaning in one's work, is truly in the realm of existential philosophers and psychologists. Indeed, one of the most prominent psychotherapies, known as Logotherapy, has at its core finding meaning in one's unique ability to contribute something to the world through work. In this way there is a reason for the need of the interrelationship between the person and the world and, as Heidegger notes, this allows the person to be genuinely "in the world."

According to Viktor Frankl, the father of Logotherapy, a human being's most basic motivation is to find meaning. For Frankl this emerges as a personal guiding myth that is centred within a cause, a reason, an aim or purpose or orientation towards a goal for which one may devote one's efforts and resources. Only in acting out this personal myth is the subjective experience of meaning found. This may be taken a step further by Jungian psychology/philosophy, which points out that each person functions within themselves in specific ways and according to "psychological types." For Jung, meaning is experienced when the myth is expressed in a form that also supports the individual's "personality type" or preferred way of being in the world. For example, I may have as my driving goal to serve the poor, however, if I am a vocal extrovert and the only way I can serve the poor is through a religious order that demands a vow of silence, I will not experience fully the deep meaning that could emerge from that vocation.

No matter the nature of one's mythic font, the individual's *opus* is a summative metamodel for experiencing meaning in everyday incidents by relating to the self and the world. This generally expresses itself in three fundamental ways: the paths of belonging (relationships), doing (meaningful engagement in activities), and understanding oneself and the world. The principles of the overall existential *opus* include intertwined fundamental meanings of human experience; the indeterminacy of cause and effect; individual differences in preferences for ways of attaining meaning; the importance of commitments in life; and life-long adaptation and changes in meaning. This overall notion provides an organizing framework that clarifies the process by which the individual is a "being" in the world and relates to the world and to one's self.

The three general aspects of relational meaning in the *opus* are interrelated in the sense that the overall experience of meaning in life is both collective and simultaneous. As with the interrelationship between one's *fons, opus* and *mortalitas*, so too there is an interrelationship between the meanings drawn from the sub-categories of relationships within each larger mythic framework.

Like every experience, the *opus* experience is a dynamic and ever flowing process. Therefore there are constantly turning points in life that hold multiple meanings for people. For example, for some people the loss of an important relationship is experienced as a loss of a sense of *belonging* that also influences their sense of being worthy of being loved (*understanding*) and the goals they set, such as pursuit of another intimate relationship (*doing*). As another example, the phenomenon of friendship is repeatedly discussed in ways that correspond to the aspects of meaning. Friends provide a sense of *belonging* and help others *do* and achieve things by believing in their capabilities and providing practical assistance. Friends also encourage self-*understanding* by validating or expanding the others' sense of self and by providing the impetus for emotional or overall mythopoeic and autopoeic growth.

Naturally, due to the variability of each person's embodied experience and their unique experience of relationships and mythopoeic structures, there is a great deal of individual differences in preferred ways of engaging in the world. The *opus* experience of some people may have a single major life theme, whereas others find meaning through a combination of themes. For some people, task-oriented activity (e.g. work, hobby, sport, or a volunteer activity) is so important and meaningful that it becomes a key life structure. Other people derive meaning in everyday life primarily through their relationships with others (belonging) or their pursuit of understanding. Of course, societal, cultural, and family influences affect these individual preferences as well.

While each person has their own preferences, there is of course the larger summative experience of the interaction between the source relationships and the *opus* ways of being in the world. It is invariable that these meta-themes are among the most powerful of relationships and form the guiding myths that enable the individual to engage even the difficult times of "being in the world." One of the most obvious integrations of this *fons/opus* interplay that forms a meta-theme for "being in the world" is found in the Woodland and Plains Cree nations of North America. Like the Cree, most of the Aboriginal nations of North America share a very clear and likely the most highly integrated mythopoeic structure of any culture of recent history.

In the traditional Cree perspective of reality, relationships are key. There is the source of all, the Great Spirit *Manitou*. However, Manitou, the Creator Spirit, is so far removed from human physical existence that one cannot please Manitou (who is the master of what happens to one in death). Therefore, what one needs are spiritual allies who can travel between the realm of men and Manitou (the spirits that live within the physical world).

These spirits, (known as *Anteyokanuks*) watch how humans live their lives, and if one honours them in this world, a spirit may choose to befriend an individual. If this happens the spirit will choose to become one's *"Powecan"* (a spiritual advocate) before Manitou. This relationship is essential to the very self-definition and autopoeic experience of the individual for it is from this relationship that one finds a name, a personal identity, in the vision quest that marks one's emergence into adulthood. It is therefore clear that the *opus* of the plains Cree is a fully integrated experience where one's *fons* in Manitou frames their active life by honouring the spirits of creation (their existential *opus*) in the hopes of receiving a *Powecan*. This then takes the Cree to the next step of interrelationship of meaning so that in the end when a Cree individual faces the issues of loss, suffering and death *(mortalitas)* there is comfort that they will have an advocate and companion to plead their case before the mighty Manitou.

From this example it is clear that the nature of one's font will form in large part one's *opus*. It is also clear that this interplay between one's source story and one's actions of being in the world helps define one's concept of the self (and overall worldview). It is also this interplay that forms one's character and moral nature, because the elusive characteristics of self-control, character and morality are all a complex nexus of the self relating to the self and also to the world and the interplay between *fons* and *opus*.

That very fragile nature of things like "character" and "morality" and the important role of accountability relationships is most clearly expressed (in a negative sense) in the horrible atrocities of Nazism. It is also clearly demonstrated in a Stanford University study on prison/prisoner relationships where one group was given control over another group, and without a clear accountability structure the abuse was stark and frightening. Even the average good, well-educated citizen, it was demonstrated, will spiral into the abyss of sexual and violent abuse when accountability relationships are absent.

To this end the *fons* myth becomes an absolutely essential factor in order for the *opus* of the individual to remain outside the control of the addictive forces of sexual abuse, violence and power. The ancient Hebrews used the Proverb "the fear of the Lord is the beginning of wisdom" to express this interrelationship of existence. The 19th century existential philosopher, Soren Kierkegaard also points out that this interplay with an accountability relationship is essential for a person to remain with any remnant of a positive character.

As Kierkegaard expresses this interplay, one can only act with character if there is an active and vital relationship between the *fons* and the *opus*. Yet, he acknowledges that some do not have an active interplay between these two forces for framing meaning and existence. One such type of person is the *student of possibility*. This person has an active and dynamic interplay between the knowledge of his/her source and how one is to live and as such recognizes the possibility of an almighty transpersonal being that observes all and may, at its will, call us to account for our actions. Such a *student of possibility* therefore recognizes that every action has a potential of being called to account and therefore the person will largely act with those selfish forces in check. Yet there is another type of person, that person is known as the *student of visible reality*. This person has a poorly developed "sense of his/her source" and therefore there is little, if any, interplay with the *opus*. For this individual, then, the only accountability relationships recognized are those of peers, society and societal authorities, such as the police. Therefore every action and choice for "being in the world" is viewed with the calculation of the odds of "getting away with," thus feeding the addictive forces of the person. Each choice in working and being in the world is viewed from the perspective of "evidence" and a "court of law" and not from the inescapable accountability relationship that guides the *student of possibility*. It is therefore clear that this nexus of relationships is essential and central in moral/character development.

The crucial interplay of these mythic structures is also essential for framing meaning, and has been in every culture in history. The very nature of the *font* myths and the character of the relationships therein will profoundly influence the role and perspective of one's *opus*. All one need do is look throughout history to see this interplay and framing process at work. For example, in the age of the Classical Greeks and the subsequent Roman Republic, much of manual work was disdained. The goal, as modeled in the *font* myths about the classical gods, was to live a life above the rigors of active work. The physical experience of "being in the world" was viewed as inferior to the ideal world of the gods.

Within the age of the Holy Roman Empire and the medieval influences of Platonic thinkers like Thomas Aquinas, the general view of the existential *opus* was two tiered. The world was divided into the Platonic spheres: the sacred spiritual life of contemplation and the secular world of labour. Contemplative "spiritual" work was considered far superior to physical earthly work. At such a time the "spiritual" work was a limited and rare privilege that could only be experienced by priests who received a "divine call." Of course this attitude can still persist, as exemplified in the often-heard phrase "full-time Christian service" and other distinctions between ministers and the lower plane of the "layman."

In theory at least, the Protestant Reformation and the Renaissance brought forth a dignity of the *opus* in the physical work and the craftsman's mode of "being in the world." Such notions like the "priesthood of all believers" attempted to clarify that in the eyes of God, there is no difference between the *opus* of the minister and that of the carpenter. As Martin Luther stated, "The works of the religious orders, however holy and arduous they may be, do not differ one bit in the sight of God, from the works of the farm labourer or the woman in the home." As John Calvin also pointed out, all work in the service and glory of God is sacred and important.

In the age of the enlightenment the momentum of the importance of every form of the *opus* was carried forward, however, it began to be separated from the guiding stories of the religious reformers. As such, the accountability relationship was transformed into a credo of personal success and personal prestige and power within the *opus*. It is this current form of thought that seems to pervade much of the first world's mode of the *opus*.

Of course, there is always the reality that all forms of work come to an end. No matter what it is that we have achieved, amassed, or otherwise succeeded in doing in this life, it will eventually fade away into the pages of antiquity. As the great Hebrew teacher stated it, "...meaningless, meaningless, for we die and all is lost." It is in this inescapable and most personal fact of life that we are reminded that a third leg is needed for the easel of meaning to remain stable as we paint the portrait of our meaningful existence.

> *One of the teachers of the law came and heard them debating. Noticing that Jesus had given them a good answer, he asked him, "Of all the commandments, which is the most important?"*
>
> *"The most important one," answered Jesus, "Is this: 'Hear, O Israel, the Lord our God, the Lord is one. Love the Lord your God with all your heart and with all your soul and with all your mind and with all your strength.' The second is this: 'Love your neighbour as yourself.' There is no commandment greater than these."*
>
> ~GOSPEL ACCORDING TO MARK 12: 28-31

Chapter Four

MORTALITAS

"As far as we can discern, the sole purpose of human existence is to kindle a light of meaning in the darkness of mere being."
~C.G. JUNG

It is a striking reality that one of the defining, un-transferable and most deeply personal experiences of life is the fact that we are living towards death. There is, of course, the question of how this knowledge of ultimate non-being will shape and influence the relationships that form meaning in life and refine our worldview. More precisely, how does the anxiety that is experienced in "being towards death" flavour one's existence and the strength of the various relationships that form the summative experience of meaning?

There are many ways of dealing with one's own inevitable mortality and how we can draw meaning from that form of our existence. One of the clearest avenues taken by existential philosophers is the notion of existential death anxiety. That is, we all tend to experience a state of being that is aware of its possibility of non-being. It is, in essence, the realization of finitude in one's being and experiences.

This apprehension in the face of the limitedness of life has caused concern for humanity down through the ages. Even the most ancient of ancients struggled deeply with this issue, only to recognize that living in a limited non-being way is the defining nature of being; that without death, human life would have little meaning and that somehow transitoriness and the experience of each person coming to an end is in some way a defining force in one's existence.

According to an ancient Sumerian myth, five thousand years ago a great warrior king named Gilgamesh walked into a tavern. The barmaid, Siduru, looked at him and said, "You look like you are near death!"

Gilgamesh stared at the barmaid and replied sullenly, "And why shouldn't I? I have battled against the curses of the gods with my friend Enkidu...and we won...but then...in the end...Enkidu died...and I do not want that fate to befall me...so I have traveled to this far eastern land to find Utnapishtim to discover the secret of eternal life."

The response of the barkeep is likely the first clear expression of the flavouring nature of the *Mortalitas*: "Gilgamesh, Gilgamesh...what are you searching for?" asked Siduru, taking on the tone of all bartenders when dealing with customers in a crisis. "You need to understand something," she said.

> "You will never find that life for which you are looking. When the gods created man they allotted to him death, but life without death they retained in their own keeping. As for you, Gilgamesh, let me give you some advice...fill your belly with good things; ... day and night, night and day, dance and be merry, feast and rejoice ... Let your clothes be fresh, bathe yourself in water, ... cherish the little child that holds your hand, ... and make your wife happy in your embrace. This is the life given to humans ."

In the end Gilgamesh discovers that what he seeks—"Immortality"—does not exist. Most scholars read this Sumerian Epic and claim that Gilgamesh *failed* in his task to find life, however, one has only to re-read the statement of Siduru to understand how wrong this is. Siduru's counsel to Gilgamesh is that human life is not the life of a god, and furthermore, true life is only found when we engage in ... life! Human life depends upon the passage of time framed within specific limits, it depends upon relationships and our engaging our own existence, and most importantly, human life is defined by the possibility, the personal and untransferable reality of one's own immanent death. The only true and authentic human life is the life that incorporates this reality into its existence *(Mortalitas)*.

Do you see what Siduru was saying to Gilgamesh? She reminds him he is human (at least partly, because Gilgamesh was said to be a descendent of the gods), so he should make that embodied existence a reality by living it. The issue is not, "What is the meaning of life?" The issue is not "eternal life." The issue is "In the face of death, how can we manage our choices and find meaning and hope?" and we received the answer in the words of a barmaid over five thousand years ago:

- *Existential Source:* Life understood in relation to the gods.
- *Existential Work*: Enjoy life by engaging it in fun, in work and in relationships.
- *Existential Meaning of Death*: Human life is defined in part by its personal finality. Death is what makes OUR existence OURS, and not that of someone else. It is also what makes every choice in life so important and precious.

Of course this ancient Sumerian myth does not encompass all that there is to one's existential *mortalitas* structure. There is also the multi-relational nexus of death and non-being. The cessation of the relating of the cellular self to itself (to ourselves within ourselves) is the objective biological death. There is also the cessation of relationships with kin and society and ways in which our own personal, subjective self is lost when these two levels of being disappear.

The nature of our existence is relational, to be sure, but it is also a dance of free choices between what is necessary and what is possible. That is, the very nature of the finitude of our existence makes every choice we make extremely important, for it sets the course and quality of our life. Yet while we are free to make choices, we are also slaves to the present circumstance that we are emerging into. Therefore life is framed in, on the one side by our past and source (after all, none of us were able to choose our parents), and on the other side, by the prison wall of death that we cannot escape. It is the limitedness of life that makes our choices so important and therefore so stressful. After all, if I could choose to study medicine for the next one hundred years and then be a painter for the following hundred years, the choice of occupation would not be so difficult. With limited time and resources the choice brings significant consequences. To choose one thing is to exclude another, hence life becomes a dance between possibility and necessity.

For example, given time and resources I could possibly have been an astronaut, however the necessity of life and the need to earn a living led to life choices that have now ruled out that possibility. So too, I may have been a famous painter (or a professional football player), yet then I would likely not have actualized my research and writing career. Due to the nature of human life, choices become extremely important. Relationships too, become extremely important, as they define the nature of our existence and the quality of our experiences.

Such choices of course have an effect upon the body as it cringes at the necessity to rule out possibilities. The result, anxiety, is what the philosophers consider to be an essential part of the embodied experience of life, for it is bodily recognizing the fact that some choices rule out what "might have been." In a sense, then, the body reacts as if we have wronged ourselves by limiting our choices. It is as if we were designed for an eternal existence, but must now somehow cram what we can into a small box that is entirely inadequate for our wants and desires.

This sense of regret is of course a result of recognizing one's mortality and must therefore be incorporated into how we live our lives. As we are making choices we are always excluding certain alternatives, and in so doing we destroy part of what we have "projected" ourselves to be becoming. Yet in the same moment a new person (a new "ME") has emerged into the present with all of its hopes, dreams and possibilities based upon a simple choice.

To ignore this double-edged sword of the nature of life choices is obviously entirely dysfunctional. Without choices we are no longer active participants in our lives, but inanimate, passive twigs that are battered about by the current of life. As such, every possibility is not saved, but instead is lost to the factors of chance and the fleeting nature of our present existence. Of course, we all are tempted to hide from the reality of our existence, engaging in a myriad of self-deception techniques to feed a fleeting need (at the expense of our larger existence). Yet when we refuse to at least engage life by exercising choices (and do it in a way that balances both our freedom and our responsibility), we deny our possibility of freely choosing towards our own future and actualizing our potential for being.

So, despite the presence of anxiety due to the finitude of life, the best life is one that approaches this fear by recognizing the power of choices and realizing that every choice means an end to certain possibilities. By adopting an attitude of courage, resolve and consideration of others, we begin to emerge as an active participant in the river of life. In adopting this stance of relating to ourselves, continually creating, choosing and letting go of possibilities for the future, we are preparing for the inevitable experience of life—letting go of ourselves, namely death.

The result ought not to be one of darkness and brooding, for to recognize that we are moving toward an indeterminable, inevitable end is to simply recognize the nature of life. To know that our existence may end (even without warning) frames every choice and relationship and moment and gives it urgency. In acknowledging this fact we are finally defining our existence as an individual, for death is personal, un-transferable and immutable. This fact can be helpful for us to prioritize and to organize relationships and refine our functional worldview.

That is to say, while relationships are important to give quality to our lives and provide them with flavour, death clarifies the order of relationships. Some relationships are shallow and fleeting, while others are more intimate and provide a deep need within ourselves for intimacy and sexuality. In these relationships we learn more about ourselves and bring out much of who we "truly are." Yet in the end, all of these relationships will be cut short and the cords left dangling. In this sense we are individuals—we are not our company, our team, our family or even our lover. We are cut off from the crowd and stand alone in our non-being of death.

At this point there remains only one possibility of relationship, only one thing that can possibly provide us with another existence. That relationship is of course, with God. As Soren Kierkegaard points out, our true and most noble calling in existence is to be a single individual that is known within that one relationship of *I and God,* or more accurately, *I in the hands of God.* This relationship is essential, then, to allow us to deal with the inevitable pain of severing from all the other relationships that will eventually end in life and in death. It is in this relationship of "I and God" (that is only clarified and revealed wholly by death) that we become an individual.

Of course, this organizing nature of death is only held in fleeting moments. Generally we cannot function with death ever before us, and thus its power to influence our authentic existence is also fleeting. The important framing power of death then is to be found in its organizing power of setting up one's mythic structure of worldview. The power of the mythopoeics of one's worldview is in its integrated nature that guides and interacts with our personal freedom to choose, while providing a guiding narrative for the choices made.

Therefore, it is clear that the *mortalitas* goes far beyond the mere action of death and entering non-being. What one is generally interested in is how this frames one's subjective experience in the present as an individual, and how that interplay between *opus* and *mortalitas* can create meaning by ordering and reinforcing certain relationships. As we push past this objective action of death to our deeper response to finitude we recognize that death and our own mortality in itself is just an obvious marker and point upon which we hinge our deep fears. Yet these fears go much deeper than just the finitude of the action of death, for what is life except relationships? So, death, in its absence of relationships, is in a way simply an ultimate expression of what we often experience in life, a faulty mode of being in the world.

More often than not we run from challenges and break relationships to avoid any manner of unpleasantness. In a small way this is in itself a state of non-being, meaninglessness and death as the relationship nexus is weaker at those points within our existence. It is here that our ontological anxiety grasps the deeper truth of our existence, obviously deeper than the external, objective fact of a biological death, but even deeper than our inward, subjective, personal fear of ceasing to be. So it may even be said that much of our anxiety does not rise within us because of death, but our fear of death arises within us because of latent ontological anxiety over how we fail to truly live genuinely within the world.

In the end however, one thing is clear. At least part of us is conscious, and consciousness by its very nature lays claim to being. Being, by its nature is dynamic and is against that which is nothingness, as much as life is against death. So too, being is a drive towards life, and since consciousness is laying claim to being, then consciousness desires being and therefore life (and logically, then, an eternal life). So too, consciousness can always pass beyond the existent (which is being), not toward its being, but toward the meaning of this being. The meaning of the being of the existent in so far as it reveals itself to consciousness is the phenomenon of being and of longing for the continuation of that phenomenon of being. Therefore, if meaning is only valid in being, and being is connected to life, then any consciousness of being will eventually need to struggle with the issue of non-being. It is in this struggle that our core self is refined and the experience of meaning is *realized* in the dynamic tension of being pulled from the present into the future, this progression eventually requiring that we be pulled towards an imagined eternal life. Therefore, meaning requires a positive stance toward being, even in the face of mortality. It knows no otherness; it never posits itself as other-than-another-being. It can support no connection with the ultimate end of non-being (even in the face of death).

That is why, even in the face of death, our conscious and self-aware self so desperately requires that we incorporate a mythic story of being into our existence and overall worldview. It is part of the very nature of being conscious and making meaning, for phenomenological and relational nothingness is meaningless. So, too, are we if we end in nothingness. As St. Paul says, *"If Christ has not risen from the dead in flesh, so that we too may rise from the dead in flesh, then we are to be the most pitied of all people"*(1 Corinthians 15).

> *The angel showed me the river of the water of life. The river was virtually transparent, with no trace of impurity. An ever-flowing fountain, it sprang from the throne of God and the Lamb, flowing down through the heart of the city. The bank of the river was framed with the tree of life, as its fruit provided for all our needs, and its leaves healed our past hurts..."Observe closely, and ponder this mystery, I am continually emerging from the past, and my reward with me...I am the Alpha and the Omega, the First and the Last, the Beginning and the End."*
>
> *...The Spirit and the bride say in one voice, "You are invited!" so let those who hear say to others, "You are invited!" Let everyone who is thirsty know that they are invited to experience the free and wonderful gift of the water, for it is pure, it is perfect, it is true life.*
>
> ~THE REVELATION OF ST. JOHN CHAPTER 22
> (Author's paraphrase of the Greek text)

Chapter Five

MENO'S PARADOX
Searching for...We Know Not What

> *"But how will you look for something when you don't in the least know what it is? How on earth are you going to set up something you don't know as the object of your search? To put it another way, even if you come right up against it, how will you know that what you found is the thing you didn't know?"*
> ~MENO'S PARADOX
> PLATO, 350 B.C.E.

One of the greatest issues that each person must struggle with when seeking "meaning" in life is found in the question posed by Meno in the writings of Plato, *"How will we know that we have found it, if we do not know what we are looking for?"* In pondering Meno's question we must recognize the systematic failure of our reliance upon scientific and empirical research to fully answer this question in a personal way. Meaning is an internal and personal experience; therefore science or philosophy and rationalism fail and are ignorant of what we seek.

Science and modern rationalism fall short as they try to understand truth as certainty. While it is true that the mind organizes or constitutes an experience of reality, we can never know reality in its fullness. Indeed, we understand only a small portion of reality, and it is ultimately organized in terms that tell us how an experience "relates to us" within a guiding mythic narrative. Our seeking for that which will satisfy our longing for meaning is not simply something that just goes on in our heads. Rather, our intentional consciousness, dialogue and resultant meaning are experienced in and through our bodies. For many of us this is difficult as we are trapped by the Platonic & Descartes' mind-body dualism and cannot break from it without resorting to physiological reductionism. However, if we think of ourselves as emerging consciousness and being only by going forth bodily into the world in search of that mysterious meaning, we are approaching the reality of our situation. The current of our person's intentional existence is then lived through the body. We are our bodies, and consciousness is not just locked up inside the head. Neither, of course then, is meaning simply experienced by the head, but rather as a full (including bodily) experience. As Katta Johanian *(The Gospel of John)* points out, "flesh" is part of our experience. Indeed, when God shared our experience in the incarnation of Christ, we have an allegory of the most excellent way of understanding and experiencing meaning *(The Word made Flesh)*. We are made of the same flesh as the world, and it is because the flesh of the body is of the flesh of the world that we can know and understand the world.

The psychologists Rollo May and Carl Jung may also have something to bring to this understanding. For May there is a simple bodily essence (a preferred pattern of relating to self within the self) that we are all endowed with that must be actualized in our existence in order for our essence of the self to be experienced in a truly meaningful way. Carl Jung observed that different people have different ways of being "in the world" and communicating with the world. These Jung called "types" and these types required certain experiences unique to that type (a context for being in the world that fit their particular mode of being in the world) in order for them to experience meaning and significance in activities. So in one way we are created for a specific task or a certain circumstance, and we must seek to find that place in order for our bodies to tell us that we are experiencing what we are searching for. One of the most popular ways of doing this is through the use of the MBTI (Myers-Briggs Type Indicator) and career counselling. When one then finds a job/environment that allows one to relate to the self and others in the preferred way, it is experienced subjectively and bodily as "meaningful." In a way, then, this is the sense of the ancient Hebrew term SHALOM which is often translated "peace" but literally means "everything in its right place." When we find our "right place" we experience peace and meaning.

The purpose, indication and perception (oh how language limits us!) of the lived meaningful existence, then, is found in our relationship to ourselves in our body and is the guide to resolving Meno's paradox. The body (including the brain) is both transcendent and immanent in its communication with itself (and therefore conscious of its own being and driven toward meaning). While we think of meaning as a philosophical answer between the dialogue of subject and object, the body interjects a third factor and reveals that a "philosophical" answer is NOT what we were looking for. Rather, what we are looking for is a right way of relating with ourselves and with others (and of course with God).

Consider for a moment how we know anything. Does a philosophical or even scientific answer ever really "satisfy" our longing for an answer? When we know something, we generally know it because we can touch it, see it, and hear it. True, we never know things (or persons) in their totality, but what we do know is almost always from an embodied perspective. Because we are flesh, we can only see a thing from a certain perspective, and yet, because we are bodily, we can also experience the thing as being more than that partial perspective. The thing exists "in itself" because it resists our knowing it with total certainty. However, the thing exists "for us" (or more accurately, "for me") because we always experience it in relation to our own body. A sofa, for example, is something to sit on. A pen is something to write with. Things allow for certain bodily engagements while closing off others. The experienced, subjective meaning for that object is created out of the bodily experience of the "I—object" relationship. In this sense meaning is both transcendent and immanent; as we interact with things a meaning is given to the experience in the form of an "in-itself-for-me" relationship. Essentially, then, we say we "understand" something or "experience meaning" when a single meaning arises out of a personal embodied phenomenological encounter of the *noumena*[10] object.

If we can grasp the notion of the "in-itself-for-me" we can fathom how experience, as it is given to us, is always a subject-object dialogue. The fact that we are flesh means that we can never experience things independent of our experience as a bodily-engaged being in the world; the meaning we bring to our perception is a perceiving which is embodied. It is by virtue of our embodiment that we can experience things as being up or down, as having insides or outsides, as being close or far away. Space is always in relation to my body as situated within the world. The same is true of time. We can never be at two places at once as a body. I am always situated in the present—on the way somewhere as having been somewhere. So too, our understanding of life's meaning and our worldview in the logical philosophical sense takes on the form of a bodily journey that must be organized in a direction. We must orient our perceived body in a psychological terrain of space that represents time. Behind us is the font from which we have sprung, presently we are walking through the path of life's choices and we will soon reach the fence of death, yet we assume that the path continues beyond the fence. So also then, our everyday experience is always in the process of becoming. Just when we are aware of things as determinate and thematic, new possibilities emerge on the horizon and the past fades away as more ambiguous. Thus, when we experience a thing within a context, this spatial-temporal context is temporary and unfolding over time, (always subject to the larger mythic terrain in which we believe) and thus subject to change (within the limits of our belief structure).

Solving Meno's paradox becomes possible with the idea of the lived bodily existence. How do we know if we've found what we are looking for? We know because our embodied experience will tell us. We will know it because the world is already loaded with meaning in relation to bodily existence. The reality

---

[10] Noumena refers to the complexity of reality as it actually is. It is far beyond our own perceptions, experiences and scientific knowledge.

we experience begins as ambiguous but always becomes more determinate as we become bodily engaged with it and as it is incorporated into our worldview. On the other hand, we do not already know what we are looking for, because the world transcends our total grasp. At any given time, the world as it is known includes not only what is revealed, but also what is concealed.

It is clear therefore that a philosophical answer is NOT that which we seek. As Meno posed the question, we reply with our own bodies and the natural process of engaging the world as we form our existence. There is no magic bullet or clear succinct answer to the question of meaning in life. It is part of the experience of being in the world and forming relationships. From this being in the world experience we begin to experience life, and form ourselves in relating with the world. Then in some mystical miraculous way, that which we seek but know not what emerges out of life.

How does this work itself out? Well, of course, it varies with one's mythic system or worldview. From the perspective of a Christian worldview we understand much of life and its meaning as being experienced within the framework of living in service as "image-bearers" of God. This includes caring for the creation and living towards ultimate and bodily salvation with God. This of course takes on an indescribably deeper meaning when one considers the reality of bodily knowing and how this ties in with meaning and the promised bodily resurrection and perfection of creation.

Meaning and knowing are in part comprehensive/summative products of proper bodily functioning and proper communication between the parts of the self as well as the interaction between the bodily self and the transcendent and immanent object. How much deeper does that meaning and knowledge go when all these areas are working "as they should" in perfect harmony and health? We can only imagine, but words of St. Paul certainly ring with a refreshed tone, "For I now know in part...for now we see only dimly, but THEN shall I know fully." (1 Corinthians 13:12, author's paraphrase).

Chapter Six

RELIGION AND LIFE
The Evidence

*"To act is to assume and to assume is to have faith.
Therefore every person is a believer,...but a believer in what?"*
~I. BAENSON

Meaning is an emerging subjective phenomenon that occurs not from any one cause but from a combination of factors resulting in a balanced communication between the different neural, bodily, social and existential structures that form that qualitative experience of meaning. It is in part relating to the "self" within the self and in part relating to our social, physical and mythical worldview environment. In light of this, one of the values of religion is clearly that it traditionally brings together many (though not all) of the ingredients necessary for this emerging subjective phenomenon.

One thing religion does is provide the flexible semi-permeable membrane of conscious/neural stimulating nutrients that allow the autopoeic process to form where there is eventually a balance of the proper and requisite relating within the self (literally *shalom*: "everything in its right place" or "a sense of peace"). So too, in meaning, some of these basic organizational features are: language (left temporal); visual and corporate maturity (cerebellum, parietal and occipital lobes); a place for the sensual/sexual (brain stem) and a narrative about where we came from (*fons, opus, mortalitas* - right temporal) and to whom we are accountable to (prefrontal), allowing the embodied self to have that full brain unified emerging subjective experience known as meaning.

While the philosophical arguments of this book may be logical, the question can still be argued, "Does this notion of the existential tripod and what appears to be the latent importance of religion hold up in the real world?" Since this book will be used on college campuses it is important to address this issue as it may apply to a student's experience, so a study was undertaken to provide a clear "real world" picture of the role of religion in creating a meaningful existence and approaching existential wellness.

Along these lines, it is clear that religion utilizes the traditional tripod for meaning. Religion provides people with a mythic worldview that addresses and draws meaning for existence from where we come from *(font)*, it defines our existence by our actions *(opus)*, and frames our existence with a mythic story about what happens when we die *(mortalitas)*.

Let us start off our discussion by taking a look at the basic psychological/existential developmental issues of university students. The ages we are typically most interested in for undergraduate education are ages 17 - 20. A modern Erikson interpretation for a person of this age suggests that the values of Identity vs. Role Confusion are very important. Here we see the student learning to manage the emerging ability to think about what others think about oneself (started in puberty), thereby causing the student to feel somewhat self-conscious. This is of course in line with Piaget's observation that they are learning to master formal operations and abstract thinking.

With regard to the ability to make meaning, Fowler identifies this time as the synthetic conventional stage. Here we see a more personal and abstract frame of meaning as the student develops personal myths about his or her own personhood. Such myths or stories often incorporate existing religious beliefs that have been reformed to focus on the uniqueness of the self and how the self relates with others. As anyone who works with this age group will recognize, it is during this age that the clarifying of the tripod of existential wellness is so very important. There are struggles with questions like, "Where do I come from?" and, "What does this mean?" (a student's story of origin).

But even more importantly, the formation of the personal myths and narratives that will form the framework of the student's *opus* occurs during this time. This is the time when students are driven by the emerging stories of what they "WILL BE" in their work life. The major driving force in their lives is WHAT THEY ENVISION themselves to be becoming in the future. It is these stories that lay the foundation for later existential growth, for they guide how the individual will understand him/her self and how he/she will encounter the inevitable difficulties, trials and issues of loss and suffering that will be faced in life. This is the theoretical framework.

The practical question in the overall university goal of forming and educating the whole person to navigate the existential paradoxes of life is whether or not organized religion has a role to play. Existentialism can be understood as the way in which an individual creates his/her meaning out of the personal schema and experiences of life. From this theoretical basis, then, the project used questions about students' experiences and the level of satisfaction with these experiences to define the parameters of our research. In essence, this study used the operational definition of existentialism as **the value of knowing where and why one fits within life.**

So also, religious well-being will be operationally defined in terms that tend to be non-sectarian and that highlight satisfaction with a relationship with a god (as god is understood by the individual), satisfaction from a meditative/prayer life and satisfaction with the faith community. These existential and religious well-being scales are published by Life Advance Corporation of Nyack, N.Y. and measure agreement to direct statements with the use of a Lickert scale.

The data used is a retrospective analysis of the data originally collected as part of a larger study to establish criterion-related validity for projective psychometrics. When the suggestion was made to present some evidence for the philosophical ideas for this book we realized that we already had the data we needed. So what we are doing here is not looking for a cause/effect relationship, but rather taking the scores of the existential well-being and religious well-being of individuals and running a correlation so that we can see the nature of the relationship. With this, then, we can look at the main effect size of this relationship. Realizing that an effect size is a fairly broad category, please let us be clear that we are just looking to discover the common domain between religious well-being and existential well-being.

The information does have some limitations, as we did not access the biographical data for the sample. Despite this limitation, when we looked at the Pearson product moment correlation coefficient between Existential and Religious Wellness:

The result for a group of 80 individuals (N-80) was an
r of +0.585 significant at the 0.01 level.

The next question was, "What is the percentage of common domain between the two variables?" We came up with a common domain of approximately **34%** between these two variables. If we consider that **34%** of existential well-being can be accounted for in and with religious factors (and issues of religious satisfaction) then it is clear *that any goal to support existential well-being within students must include support for the student's religious life.*

By supporting religious life in students we are supporting the construction of the traditional tripod of forming a meaningful existence: *Fons, Opus, Mortalitas*. However, let us be clear; this does not mean that any particular religious structure is better than any other. It does not mean that a good religious life is assurance of existential wellness. Rather, all we can say is that there does seem to be a partnership between the two, and to limit the one will invariably hamper the development of the other. Why? Simply because there is this massive common domain (what we consider to be the mythopoeic worldview) between the two variables. So, if colleges are to be in the business of fostering an individual's ability to navigate the inevitable issues of life—from loss and suffering to existential paradoxes—then we must make allowance for the formation of the religious life of the individual.

In addition to our findings, other research has been found to support our conclusions about this topic. As the Gibbs (1978) study reveals, during periods of serious adjustment spiritual values are essential in reducing anxiety. In the Hackey and Sanders (2003) meta-analysis there was also shown a positive relationship between religious life and psychological adjustment. Laurencelle (2002) also notes that incorporated internalized religious stories support an overall sense of well-being and increase stress management capabilities.

So, from an existential development perspective at least, faith-based communities, groups and relationships are important for the overall balancing of life, overall wellness, adjustment, and just simply living a life.

It becomes clear through the research that there is significant power within the mythopoeic support found in religion, for it is clearly a powerful tool for helping people form their own personal stories. However, we must also be mindful of the danger of faith-based programs that can crush individual stories. In this sense we can embrace religion while still recalling the mantra of St. Anselm, *"Reforma Reformanda"* (the church reformed and always in the process of reforming).

Chapter Seven

EXPERIENCING THE TRIPOD
A Guided Imagery Exercise

"Praise the Lord, O my soul; all my inmost being, praise his holy name. Praise the Lord, O my soul, and forget not all his benefits – who forgives all your sins and heals all your diseases, who redeems your life from the pit and crowns you with love and compassion."

~PSALM 103: 1-4

In a very simple way the issue of bodily experiencing meaning can be grasped through the mythopoeic process of guided imagery. Please take a moment to find a quiet place and ask a friend to help you by reading aloud the following pages in a slow, quiet, deliberate voice. In this way, you can experience a small hint of what relational and bodily experienced meaning is like.

ഔര

    In your imagination, go to a quiet place on a high hill, and from that high hill you can look into your past...year after year surrounds this hill...spread out for you to see in the valley below...
    Look down and identify your greatest achievements...those things that everyone applauds you for...feel the adoration of the crowds and the congratulations of friends.
    But now...as you stand upon the top of that mountain, pick up a mask that lies at your feet...it is the mask of a fierce and vengeful "god" (it won't be hard to do...you've picked up this mask many times before as you have played this role). Notice how the world looks so different through this mask...feel your warm breath against the mask. Now let your gaze survey the valley below.
    Take note of some of the glaring imperfections you are guilty of:
    Your manipulation of others...

Mistakes of choice...
Self pity...
Lack of courage...
Secret deals made between you and your own dark desires...

As you survey the valley...notice all the blemishes in your character, feel that feeling of becoming extremely displeased with yourself; and, like an angry god...punish yourself...stop the rain from falling upon that once lush and green valley...watch it wither and become dry and dusty under the heat of the day.

Then...punish yourself some more...block the sun...with dark, deep clouds...allowing the cold and darkness to encompass the valley of your past life.

Observe how all that grows in the valley shrivels up...
Feel saddened by all the lack of life that lies below you...
Feel your present hopelessness as well...

Then...in the midst of the darkness...see a strong beam of light break through...falling upon a section of the valley...and where that light hits...life instantly springs back. Then as the light grows feel a sweet gentle rain give relief to the parched land...

Suddenly you feel a hand upon your shoulder...and a voice whispering in your ear..."It is not for you to play god"...a hand slides the mask off your face and you see a face...thin and long...a bearded face...with a smile as He speaks.

"My command was this: love your enemies, pray for those who persecute you."

Let Him speak the good news to you.

As He talks to you, watch God's sun and rain make the valley good and green again...

As you watch, let Jesus point out some of the interesting scenery in the panorama of your past life...let Him praise you for the ways you've grown so far, despite your imperfections...let Him remind you that it was God's sun and rain—His constant presence and assurance—that has helped you through it all...let Him warn to be gentle with yourself as He is, and has always been, with you ...then sit on the hill for a moment...in silence...as you again look upon your life...slowly moving position to see the different parts...as you gaze farther and farther into your past.

You see your old school...your first experience...kindergarten...and you think of your teacher...you stand...dust yourself off and head down the hill toward the school...the school of your past. You enter the door...your perspective is so different now...things are so much smaller...but the sounds...the smells...are all the same...you step into the classroom and walk into the room...slowly turn to take in the whole scene...and then sit on the floor.

EXPERIENCING THE TRIPOD: A Guided Imagery Exercise

You think back to a time in the past year when you did a "good thing" for a person. Perhaps gave money...or supported a good cause...or volunteered to work...or helped someone. Think of this...as you look at all the little chairs that sit within this kindergarten room... As you look at a chair let the image of the child that bullied you in school form...next to that person...let one who gossiped about you form in the next chair...slowly go around the room...and let all the chairs fill with people...talking about you...and your faults...gossips and rumours that hurt you. Remember what they said about you and how they said it.

Imagine them sitting in those chairs facing you repeating those vicious slurs, vicious tongues, mean faces, even declaring judgment on your generous acts of kindness...

Feel the sting of their words. As you do, you feel yourself begin to shrink...

Feeling smaller and smaller...as helpless now as a kindergarten child in the middle of this ring of bullies.

The door opens...and suddenly everyone goes silent as they turn to the door...and Jesus enters...slowly walking into the room...the angry faces turn to faces of fear as Jesus walks slowly into the room...around the room...around you...touching each accusing voice as they disappear in a wisp of air...until only the two of you remain...you...a little child...sitting upon the floor...and Jesus...who reaches down and takes your hand...and gently helps you to your feet...and walks you to the door.

As you step out of the kindergarten room you find yourself in a field...a lovely meadow that until this moment only existed in your imagination. The gentle afternoon sun is warm on your shoulders...you smile and relax and feel the deep rhythm of your breathing.

But it is so hard to forget what just happened...and you again start to think about those that criticize you...only this time it is a person who criticized you recently. As you turn in the beautiful meadow...you see this person walking towards you...you feel the anxiety rising within yourself but try to remain calm.

Let this critic point out your faults in their customary way...

Listen to what they are saying...in the way that it usually is said...listen without defensiveness.

Then from the corner of your eye you see another person walking toward you...this one is a friend of yours...one from whom it is easy to accept advice.

Let your friend point out the same shortcomings of yours...hear those specific words...as they speak kindly...caring for you...but acknowledging the truth of your critic's words as well...

Finally, let both friend and critic shake hands...and walk away...out of sight...

EXPERIENCING THE TRIPOD: A Guided Imagery Exercise

In silence, ask God to give you courage to improve on those aspects of your life that these two people have mentioned...and that you have discovered need improvement...

Next you see a wooden basket at your feet and instinctively you know what it is for...your pain...your hurt...what others have done to you...and what you have done to others. You lift the empty box and walk through the valley...starting with all the hurts of yesterday...picking up those hurts and placing them in the basket. Then you continue on...to the pains of last year...again picking them up and placing them in the basket...you wander through the valley of your past...in the midst of its beauty...finding all the ugly parts that stick out...a moment of desire that you are ashamed of here...a lost goal there...a time that you were hurt...everything being placed in that basket...back...into your childhood...to the earliest hurt you remember...there it lies at the base of a rocky cliff at what appears to be the end of the valley.

Yet...you realize that it is not the end...for inbetween the rocks is a craggy path leading up a hill...and you start up...basket in hand...as the path becomes rockier and the wind begins to swirl around you as you arrive at the top of the hill... you are alone.

The hill is unprotected...the scenery is severe, foreboding...you look down and notice that the clothes you wear are not enough to keep away the bite of the wind.

Let the harshness of it be as much as you can bear...then let it be a little more...

On that unprotected hill, think of your favourite temptation to give up...something that you are holding with you in the basket...what is your weakness?

Remember a recent time when you felt grief because of these feelings...or because of the death of a loved one,...or because of physical pain...or anxiety...or frustration in life...whatever.

Feel, once again, the urge to "put blinders on"...to settle down in the sadness...be oblivious, once more, to life around you...

Feel, once again, so sad that it is almost too much to bear...then feel it even worse....

When it becomes unbearable, and as you curl up from the pain you hear a series of ragged breaths...behind you...you cannot look...and then there is a scream... "My God, my God...why have you forsaken Me?" You close your eyes...and put your hands over your face to block out all the light...and all goes silent...the wind has stopped...

Slowly you pull your hands away from your eyes and look around...you are sitting upon a rock still...but the scene has changed...no longer are you on a hill...you are now in a dark cave...cold...damp...and as you look to your left you see a body. This is no cave...this is a tomb...where a dead corpse is lying.

You are here...in this tomb...and somehow...in some way...experience being there with the dead...and as you look at the face of this dead man...there is a twinge of recognition...and in that stillness and darkness...there is a breath that breaks the silence...Jesus has passed over the Sea of Death and is now forever secure in His new life...He sits up...and turns and smiles at you ...holding out both His hands...as if to take you by the hands...

You hesitate for a moment to extend both hands...thinking you cannot manage with your basket of hurts...but then you look down...at your arm...where your basket was supposed to be...and you realize it is gone...it is gone...and the darkness of the cave has now been transformed with the light and warmth of that first hill...as you extend your free hands to Jesus...

There you stand with Jesus...hand in hand...facing each other...on the mountain that overlooks the valley of your whole life... You are with Jesus...as He lifts his eyes to heaven to praise God, His Father...feel the sun break through the clouds ...

Stand in awe...as you see the most brilliant rainbow develop over the valley...right before your eyes...so close you can almost touch it...As you watch...let Jesus speak to you of the meaning of the rainbow and of His Resurrection...how...your basket is gone forever in this life of the resurrection...then hear the words of the Psalmist as finally you understand these words:

> *MY GOD...MY GOD...WHY HAVE YOU FORSAKEN ME?*
> *Why are you so far from me, so far from the groaning of my spirit.*
> *I feel so alone...but in you Oh God I trust.*
> *I am but a worm to those who surround me and they mock me...and they mock my trust in you...I am poured out like water before them and my body is broken and my will melts, my strength and my mouth are dry...and the evil men encircle me and cast lost for my clothing...they have pierced my hands and feet...and yet I trust in you.*
> *For you will not forget your beloved children...I know that you give a gift of forgiveness so that I will be satisfied...so that hearts and lives are healed forever...and your good news will be preached to a people yet unborn...you have done it."*
> *The Lord is my shepherd, I shall not be in want. He makes me lie down in green pastures, he leads me beside quiet waters, he restores my soul. He guides me in paths of righteousness for His name's sake. Even though I walk through the valley of the shadow of death, I will*

fear no evil. For you are with me. Your rod and your staff they comfort me.

You prepare a table before me in the presence of my accusers and anoint me with oil; my cup overflows...

Surely goodness and love will follow me and I will be with the Lord...Forever.

For there is nothing that can separate us from the Love of God that is in Christ Jesus our Lord.

Chapter Eight

KNOW THYSELF
Your Sacred Autobiography

Who Am I?

They tell me, I would bear the days of misfortune equably, smilingly, proudly,

Like one accustomed to win. Am I really all that?

Or am I only what I know of myself, restless and longing and sick,

Like a bird in a cage, struggling for breath, as though hands were compressing my throat, yearning for colours, for flowers, for the voices of birds, thirsting for words of kindness, for neighbourliness...powerlessly trembling for friends at an infinite distance, weary and empty at praying, at thinking, at making,

Faint, and ready to say farewell to it all? Who am I?
Whoever I am, you know O God,

I am yours.

~DIETRICH BONHOEFFER

It is so very true that we know ourselves only in relation to ourselves within ourselves and in relationship with others. So in order to truly engage life and have a sense of self and therefore self-worth and meaning one must actively delve into the stories that guide and shape and represent these relationships. As we consider our own personal mythic stories the self and one's worldview emerges from the nexus of relationships. Let us therefore take some time and practice the creating of our own myths by looking back into our memories to(re)-create the events that have shaped who we are. **Take some time to write them down.** In so doing we can glean much about ourselves and find a firmer grasp for the rudder that guides us into our future.

In writing out your own history give some thought to what the design of your life is (I suggest that you also include your family of origin back four generations). Patterns and plots keep the story moving and answer the *"What happens next"* questions. These themes set up the scene, move us through the dilemmas faced by the character (you) and bring us to a final resolution. In considering the mythopoeic plot for your own autobiography, ask yourself where the story begins (what is your source...on all its levels) and where does the story end (both at the present and in your ultimate mortality). Is there a lesson(s) that you can learn from the plot of your own story? What parts are most significant for you, and what parts have you chosen not to include in the story?

Once you have given some thought to the overall outline and theme of your autobiography, proffer contemplation to the character (you). What do you choose to reveal in this narrative? What desires and inner dialogues that you have had with yourself have you omitted from this story (and how does this influence how you portray yourself)? What are the other characters that intersect with you and locate you within these associations? Also consider the nature of these relationships and the themes that emerge; is it attraction or repulsion, friend or enemy, peace or war?

While contemplating the nature of the relationships, be sure to convey key moods that have shaped your life. It may be the bittersweet nature of a relationship with an authority figure, or the joy and heartbreak of your first love. Whatever the nature, ensure that the moods of the key moments are captured within your story. This will help you to set up a good first draft of your narrative.

Of course, because we are relational creatures, an autobiography written only for our own eyes limits its benefit. Therefore, please share your autobiographical story with someone else. It may be in the context of a classroom, where you exchange autobiographical stories for a class assignment, or in a spousal relationship in order to revive the spark. Whatever the context, read the other person's story with empathy and confidentiality, and at the same time ask questions that will help that person clarify who they are to you. This whole process is of course valuable not only for the other person, but also for your own self-knowledge.

We are empathic creatures that naturally have an interest in others, for in knowing others we discover more about ourselves. We learn that knowing ourselves emerges from learning about others, and we experience that others are like us in basic ways. We are all, for example, full of dispositions, interests, desires, questions, insecurities and unmet longings. Therefore, by sharing the myths of others we engage in the activity that declares our solidarity, our common humanity, and therefore reinforces our own value.

Of course, there is a skill that must be learned when listening to or reading the other's story. It must be experienced and understood in "their" terms and therefore we must exercise the empathic process of "walking in their shoes." This will require you to draw upon your own similar experiences and to reform them into a context similar to that described by the other. It is clear that there will be both similarities and differences between your experiences and the author, and both are educative.

Once you have had the opportunity to share with another, and have discussed your story (and theirs), it is time to again revisit your narrative for life. There are some key issues to keep in mind when you go back and re-create your autobiography: What events were most important in life? What stories best reflect who I am? What is your sacred story? How are you connected to the eternal? How is this connection expressed in your community? What is your belief statement or creed (or do you even have a creed)? What elements of organized religion are in your life and how does this inform you about who you are?

This brings us to the second level of your mythopoeic process, where we move from your public self to your sacred and meaningful self.

In reflecting upon the sacred self we are recognizing the religious/mythic stories that organize and give life a sense of order. The truth is that everyone has a sacred self, whether they are Buddhist, Muslim, Hindu or Christian. Indeed, even the atheist or agnostic that swears they, "do not have a religious hair on their head" are nevertheless guided by a sacred self (in the form of their worldview). The reality is that whatever is of primary concern to someone is their god (as Martin Luther put it), and everyone has an underlying faith (even if it is in Budweiser and Football). Accordingly, then, everyone has a sacred self that they rely upon to give their life order and direction.

In considering the sacred self and in re-creating your autobiography it is important to give consideration to the rituals and rites that are performed (and that your parents performed). For the Christian these are things like partaking in the Lord's Supper/Eucharist and celebrating seasons of the Christian calendar like Advent, Christmas, Easter etc. It may also involve practices like bowing, kneeling or folding one's hands in prayer. All of these things contribute to how one relates to the larger worldview and forms one's sacred self.

Religious/sacred issues are also beliefs and not simply practices, so the issue of one's creed is also important. It is therefore important to recognize where one is located within a community, what the creed of that community is, and whether you agree or disagree (and why) with that creed. There is of course the essential issue of forming and refining one's personal creed. Generally creeds are systematic statements of the central beliefs of the tradition. In the

Christian tradition the old Roman creed popularly known as the Apostles' Creed is the cornerstone repeated in services around the world:

> I believe in God the Father Almighty, maker of heaven and earth. I believe in Jesus Christ, his only son our Lord who was conceived by the Holy Spirit, born of the Virgin Mary, suffered under Pontius Pilate, was crucified, dead and buried. On the third day he arose from the dead. I believe in the Holy Spirit, the holy catholic church, the communion of the saints, the forgiveness of sins, the resurrection of the body, and the life everlasting, Amen.

Give thought to the beliefs that are central to how you understand the universe, these are generally relational, and in the end form an individual's sacred creed.

Finally, one last area that is essential to understanding the sacred self is community. What community do you belong to and how do these relationships (with like minded people) reinforce and challenge what you do and how you view the world? What is the moral code and standard of expectations of this community and how does this either pressure you to consider the welfare of others, or direct you toward self-indulgence? What is the history of your beliefs and community? Are you a member of a long catholic tradition or a convert to Homer Simpsonism (*a.k.a. beer and donuts*), and how does this locate you within human history? Also, what is the character of this sacred context? Is it active and engaging and positive or is it repressive and constricting? How does this influence your sense of self and how you exist in the world?

The autobiography of your sacred self will hopefully provide you with a chance to again share your story with someone else. In this story you can find how you are constructed by ceremony, creed, community and character in order to emerge as a unique and valued individual. In so doing, hopefully you will be able to answer the question asked by Dietrich Bonhoeffer, "WHO AM I?"

II.

Meeting Different Worldviews

The following are imaginary monologues created by the author to introduce you to some people and their various worldviews. Some of the individuals are real and others are not. However, none of the presentations are meant to be accurate reflections of the beliefs held by the individuals. The purpose of this section is exclusively to introduce the reader to the various possible ways of apprehending the world.

> *"The world is.. the natural setting of, and field for, all my thoughts and all my explicit perceptions. Truth does not "inhabit" only "the inner man," or more accurately, there is no inner man, man is in the world, and only in the world does he know himself."*
>
> ~MAURICE MERLEAU-PONTY (1945)

WORLDVIEW OF THE NEW ORDER
K. Rajaratman (Age: 89)

I live in what was once called the city of Madras, in Tamil Nadu, India. In the 1990's the name of the city was changed to Chennai, but I still prefer the old name of Madras (it is what I grew up with). I will tell you a little about myself and then I would like to share with you my passion. I am a child of Hindu parents (a lower class we call the DALIT's—a Sanskrit term that means "the broken twig") and I was raised in the city of Chennai, India. I studied at Madras Christian School and in my teens started to seek an understanding of Christianity. In my late teens and early 20's I studied economics at the University of Madras and completed my Ph.D. at the London School of Economics. I spent most of my life teaching economics at the University of Madras graduate school before I retired and founded the *Center of Research on the New Economic World Order*, a government sponsored academic think-tank in Chennai. This is my passion!

Let me share with you a little about how I see the world as a person interested in service of the poor, as both a Christian and an economist.

> *God blessed them and God said to them, "Be fruitful and multiply and fill the earth and subdue it and have dominion over the fish of the sea and over the birds of the air and over everything that moves upon the earth.*
> ~GENESIS 1: 28

I see the world as being fairly steady and predictable throughout its history up until the year 1900 (I am speaking in economic terms...since this is my passion). In fact, when I was born I would still consider this part of what I can call the "old order" because the world has changed so drastically in my lifetime. Today it is really difficult to grasp the sheer magnitude of the growth of both wealth and population. Let me put it into perspective—from the beginning of time until 1950 the world economy grew from nothing to a total economy of approximately $4 trillion (US currency). Compared with what is happening now, it grows by this same amount in only TEN YEARS!

For many in the world this means that earthly life has taken on what people one hundred years ago would describe as "heavenly life." As such, the issues of death and the life after death have been displaced by a pursuit of wealth and success like in no other time in history. This also means, of course, that the rich do not understand the poor and the poor do not understand the rich (because the gulf between the two is greater than at any time in human history). The result is that the rich, who live in a heaven "par excellence," have the power to exploit the poor and turn their lives into hell on earth (without even intending to do so).

I am old enough to remember Mohandas Ghandi speak of a world where "there is enough for everyone's need but never enough for everyone's greed." I did not realize the power of those words at the time, but now in my old age I am horrified at the power of the truth within those words. Oh sure, Jesus said we will "always have the poor" but the gap between the rich and the poor has now reached unprecedented proportions.

Let me give you a few examples. In the world today we have approximately three hundred billionaires and five million millionaires, and in general these families control the fate of three-quarters of the world. In that latter three-quarters of the world (some five billion people) there are two hundred million who live under ox-carts or in city garbage dumps. Contrast this with the average North American who is concerned primarily with weight-loss (last year North America spent $9 billion on special diets) while the world's poorest one billion people suffered from stunted growth from being under-nourished, and an additional billion people have to drink and bathe in water contaminated with parasites and bacteria.

If we consider things like infectious diseases or suffering by being a refugee, again, people in Western Europe or North America are clueless as to the mess that they in part have created. Last year 42% of global deaths were caused by infectious diseases and 99% of these occurred in the developing world. Of course, this would not be so bad if the industrialized countries did not continue to arm factions to play their subtle games of intrigue with the rest of the world. The result? Well imagine the entire nation of Canada living in tents as war refugees. Let me contrast how the world has changed in my lifetime: In 1960 the global number of refugees was 1.4 million and this number has risen steadily year after year until now we are facing a global crisis of thirty million refugees globally. My point is, how often do we hear of these issues on the evening news? Whether I am watching TV in Chennai, London, Rome or Washington, I hear none of it.

Of course I do not want to sound like a bitter old man, but I am a realist. The world in my lifetime has shifted into two very distinct classes: 1. The powerful minority and; 2. The powerless majority. The thing that is so striking is that the rich do not even realize who they are, and often they are Christians, so it is not so much a conscious attempt to make a mess of the earth so much as it is blissful ignorance. Let me illustrate what I mean.

I would expect that almost every businessman in North America or Europe has heard the Biblical parable contrasting the rich man with poor Lazarus, who was destined to collect the crumbs from the rich man's table for his survival. As an economist who lives and works with the third world this is how I see the move towards globalization of the marketplace. The Group of Seventy-Seven countries—that is, the poor of the world—survive on the crumbs of that fall from the rich Group of Seven (or I suppose what is now called the G-8 when we include Russia), the affluent countries.

Thanks to Globalization (which was supposed to ensure the flow of capital and goods between countries) the world economy has turned into a mechanism that keeps the poor seventy-seven countries barely alive in order to serve the G-8 interests. An example of the WTO hegemony is the case of the USA obtaining a patent on turmeric products. In India, the use of turmeric, neem leaf and many other herbs is a matter of the common knowledge that forms part of the country's wealth. Illiterate men and women are aware of and have access to the use of these herbs. But the WTO mechanism was used to obtain a patent on these herbs in the US, thus making it a punishable offence in India to patent their use. For instance, the use of the vast natural resources of the neem tree in India can be blocked by a smart country through the instrumentality of the WTO. In essence then, hundreds of millions of individuals who use neem products in home-based businesses are subject to prosecution under WTO rules. The ridiculous thing about it is that these are people who have a household income of less than $300 year US who are being prosecuted by multinational corporation lawyers (who wear shoes that cost more than a family's annual income). You can see that this cannot lead to a common global good.

So what are the possible results of this trend? Well at present I see three options for the twenty-first century. The first is more of the same where the silent majority are given a smaller and smaller share of the shrinking natural resources like clean water, food and fuel (at present the poorest 20% of the world's population have only 1.6% of the world's wealth). If they remain silent and the trend continues they will die (I am speaking here of 1.5 billion people).

The second option is where I see the trend moving (unfortunately for everyone involved). This second option is where the silent and poor begin to strike back through radical factions. This means rallying around religious icons and individuals to bind people together that have only one thing in common (an empty stomach). The desperation will express itself in terms of suicide bombers and iconic violent acts in order to catch the attention of first world. Of course the events of Sept. 11th (2001) gave a clear message along these lines, but the first world totally missed the desperate cry of the poor (made vicariously through the acts of the terrorists) in the attacks upon the World Trade Center. The poor of the world sent a message but it was not heard. If ever it is heard I see hope for the future in the third option.

The third option is the hope that the Christian Church in the First World will hear the cry of the poor and oppressed and act. Biblically, of course, according to the historical teachings of the Christian church and according to Jesus who died on the cross at the hands of the priests and the state for the sake of the poor millions, the Church in any country has no choice except to take the side of the exploited, be it in one's own country or outside. Otherwise the Church is an abettor of the crimes of the state and the multinational corporation.

I am an optimist, but also a realist. I am an old man and I do not expect to live long enough to find out which option this generation will choose...I can only teach, preach and pray. In my heart I expect that we will continue to spiral into the cycles of oppression and environmental abuse that are present today and that are seen in the apocalyptic imagery of the Revelation of St. John. I will not be surprised if the "global war on terror" increases as people become more desperate, and the first world becomes more fearful (in its ignorance of the real issues). However I do have a hope, that when things are the darkest Christ will return in all His glory and "cut the days short" as Jesus says in the gospel according to Matthew. Then we will finally see justice and peace and feasting for all. I look forward to that day...for it will be the day of my resurrection.

Worldview of the Foolish
Erasmus of Rotterdam (circa 1500)

My friends, I have been doing a lot of traveling of late and much thinking. Of course I am not familiar with your time as I predate you by some five hundred years, yet I believe that I have much by way of insight and humour that you might be able to grasp and appreciate. I wish to share with you a little about my worldview, but I hope to do it in a fun and fanciful way. I am a Christian scholar and educator who lives and works in the Holy Roman Empire. Of course, in my time the Turks are pressing forth against the people of God and this makes life difficult, yet we survive. Let me therefore share with you some fun prose about the stupidity of people and the folly of human life.

I think that idiocy gets a bad rap! I see already that you are grimacing with disdain, with your brows furrowed in your enlightened self-righteous indignation. You folks are indeed like the changing of the seasons so fickle are your thoughts on this issue. Let us be honest for a moment shall we? We all love idiocy.

Now listen carefully to what I mean. Do not listen with those ears that you carry to church, but with those you use to hear the gossip about your neighbour. Indeed it would be best if you pull out the large elephant ears that you use to listen to rumours about your priest or your politician or your boss, for those ears miss nothing at all. Indeed, if I fail to speak those ears will whisper such wonderfully thrilling things to your mind that I will hardly have to do any of the work at all!! Oh how wonderful are those ears!

Now naturally you should not expect from me, when speaking in the defence of idiocy, to speak in the manner or a rhetorician or political leader. I will of course speak only in the tones of curious trifles and with the thrilling laughter of jugglers and buffoons, but why not? That is the best kind of talk after all! The talk that is meaningless and concerned only with complaining about the state of things, while sipping a little ale—would you not agree that of all the types of words that one can utter, the best are those that one mutters while one's lips are wet with alcohol?

Here is the truth, so far as I can tell. Idiocy is not a concept, but it is a person. Idiocy has legs, and arms and a mouth, and of course those giant ears! He is of course not a god, but is still of noble birth, hailing back to his origins on the Fortunate Islands. His father was called Midas (and if you know him you will understand much about Idiocy himself). Of course his family life was not stable—as a child he would often suckle the jolly nymphs. This was not his fault but in part due to his mother's impish nature, her name being Sycophancy (if you knew her you would understand much about him).

As you can see, Idiocy has little to do with how he is, as he is largely the result of his parents' nature. Of course we love him all the same, we invite him into our homes, we embrace him at the dinner table and invite him out on the town at the end of a hard week's labour. Oh but we all know the best time to have him as a companion! Yes indeed, Sunday morning! What better breakfast guest could one ask for than to begin the week in his presence! Indeed did not Jesus himself thank him for concealing the mystery of salvation? Of course! So why would we not have him as our ever-present companion?

Well I hope that I have not offended any of the women in the audience by being so audacious as to leave out your so fair a sex. But it is true my ladies that Idiocy is of a masculine nature. So sad, but true it is that we cannot help but be sexist in our talk of such a noble companion. Yet in the end we can all agree that whether we like it or not, men dominate, therefore idiocy shall always be at the right hand of empires and nations and places of power. What a joy and assurance this is. The end.

WORLDVIEW OF THE ROMAN CATHOLIC PRIEST
S. Titus – USA (Age: 71)

What is a worldview?

I recently put this question to my parish and received many blank looks in return. I wasn't surprised. If asked the same question, I would have had the same puzzled response. I continued by saying that everyone has a worldview, but most people aren't aware of it. Since they do have a worldview, shouldn't they know something about it?

Oftentimes Roman Catholics fail to consider and contemplate their presuppositions and beliefs. Sadly, many go through the motions of life without applying Catholic doctrine to every facet of their lives. But if those beliefs do not permeate their thoughts and deeds they risk failing to be disciples of Jesus Christ and holy children of God. While a Catholic worldview must be organic and cohesive, it is made up of specific elements, each worthy of attention. Here, then, are the key attributes of a Catholic worldview. Although this list is not exhaustive, I believe these elements are essential.

ONE GOD: There is only one God and he is Other. The first commandment was "I am the Lord your God . . . You shall have no other gods before Me" (Deut. 5:6, 7). Consider that some Catholics flirt with or embrace views of God that violate the first commandment. Some harbor pantheistic tendencies: God is an impersonal force that is in everything. For others God is a good luck charm, someone to call upon in times of need. All of us are tempted at times to say that there is one God, but then in our hearts and lives seek after the gods of power, money, fame, and position. "These empty idols make their worshippers empty," states the Catechism, "Those who make them are like them; so are all who trust in them."

GOD IS THREE: The Catechism declares: "The mystery of the Most Holy Trinity is the central mystery of Christian faith and life. It is the mystery of God in Himself. It is therefore the source of all the other mysteries of faith, the light that enlightens them." Jews and Muslims believe that God is One, but only Christians assert that this One God is three Persons. This great mystery provides clues to the meaning of all reality. God is Perfect Relationship, the epitome of love and communion. Because of this Trinitarian love all things were created with mankind specially created "in the image of God" and endowed with free will. To think of the Trinity as a just another dogma misses that the Trinity is the source—and focus—of all things, including our salvation.

GOD WAS FLESH: "...and the Word was God" (Jn. 1:1). Being Catholic is to be immersed in the fact that God became man, that the Eternal Creator entered time and space, ate and drank, suffered and died. "Belief in the true Incarnation of the Son of God is the distinctive sign of Christian faith," teaches the Catechism, "'By this you know the Spirit of God: every spirit which confesses that Jesus Christ has come in the flesh is of God.'"

THE CHURCH: A great gift of the Second Vatican Council was a renewed understanding of the Church as the family of God, a supernatural communion with the Trinity and with one another brought about by God's grace. This was a restoration of a biblical truth occasionally pushed to the side in recent centuries. "God created the world for the sake of communion with his divine life, a communion brought about by the 'convocation' of men in Christ, and this 'convocation' is the Church. The Church is the goal of all things..." Having a worldview that is ecclesial, or Church-centered, means envisioning all of humanity having communion with God as a part of His family, the Church.

WORD AND SACRAMENT: The communal worship of the Church reflects a profound recognition of who God is and who we are in relation to Him—and therefore to each other. Liturgy is an entrance into the kingdom of God here on earth. The Byzantine Divine Liturgy begins with the priest exclaiming: "Blessed is the Kingdom of the Father and the Son and the Holy Spirit." Thus, the Catechism declares that "In the liturgy of the New Covenant every liturgical action, especially the celebration of the Eucharist and the sacraments, is an encounter between Christ and the Church." Catholics should see liturgy and the sacraments as truly cosmic events, transforming creation and bringing it closer to that final day when God will "be all in all" (1 Cor. 15:28).

THANKSGIVING: To look at the world "Eucharistically" means several things: God dwells among mankind. God's love for the world knows no bounds. True life comes through death and sacrifice. Christ gives Himself to us so that we can give ourselves to Him and for others. The Catechism teaches that "The Eucharist is 'the source and summit of the Christian life.' For in the blessed Eucharist is contained the whole spiritual good of the Church, namely Christ himself, our Pasch." The transformation of this world began with the Incarnation and continues through the Church as sinners are changed into holy saints through regular communion with the Risen Lord. Do we as Catholics live as though we consume the actual body, blood, soul, and divinity of God? The Catholic Faith is not a private religion meant to be celebrated behind closed doors. It is open to the world although not of this world, active in the world, but not belonging to the world.

TRADITION AND SCRIPTURE: For Catholics the Word of God is "a single sacred deposit" consisting of both Sacred Tradition and Sacred Scripture. These two are like a mirror, the Catechism explains, in which "the pilgrim Church contemplates God." While many Christians look only to the Bible, Catholics view reality through the lens of both Scripture and Tradition. Scripture divorced from Tradition leads to subjective, individualistic beliefs. Embracing Tradition is not merely an acknowledgement of the past, but a trust in the work of the Holy Spirit, who continues to speak to and through the Church.

ORDER: A Catholic Worldview is hierarchically ordered in several ways. Hierarchy means "order." Catholics should see the God-given order that exists in correct doctrine, authority, and relationships. The Catechism teaches, "In Catholic doctrine there exists an order or hierarchy of truths, since they vary in their relation to the foundation of the Christian faith." This does not mean that some teachings are more true than others, but that certain truths—such as the Trinity and the Incarnation—demand more of our attention and consideration than others. There is a proper order to truth; if this order is not followed than truth atrophies or is misunderstood.

HISTORICAL: On one hand history validates the truthfulness of Catholicism, and on the other the Catholic Faith explains the meaning of history: "Christ is Lord of the cosmos and of history. In Him human history and indeed all creation are 'set forth' and transcendently fulfilled." Catholics can look at history as a source of truth, encouragement, and hope. Studied with the eyes of faith, history demonstrates God's love for humanity, first in the Incarnation and then in the lives of the saints, and shows that God is patiently working to call mankind to Himself. A Catholic Worldview that does not appreciate history will be anemic and only partially formed.

PRINCIPLED: The moral life is not simply about being good, but about being ordered to truth and holiness, which both come from God. Morality must be rooted in Jesus Christ.

WORLDVIEW OF THE LIVING EARTH
K. Ahenakew
Aboriginal Leader and Educator – Canada

I consider it of utmost importance that there be recognition of Aboriginal worldviews. There is a slow but gradual movement within academic circles to include the knowledge and worldviews of Aboriginal peoples in conversations; particularly concerning the environment. Nevertheless, we must remember that we still have a long way to go before Aboriginal philosophies are academically and socially recognized as valid and valuable sources of knowledge.

In the past (and in some cases even today) discussions concerning Aboriginal cultures were relegated to the sphere of anthropology, and by relation, ethnology. This, in part, was due to ethno-centric beliefs held by the dominant societies of North America with regards to Aboriginal peoples. Subsequent to systematic governmental policies of genocide and assimilation, the late nineteenth century saw a vast army of anthropologists and ethnologists entering into 'Aboriginal Country'. They recorded and catalogued the cultures and rituals of what were then considered the 'vanishing Aboriginals' of the Americas. Anthropological and ethnological research of the late nineteenth and early twentieth centuries was mainly concerned with the collection of the material culture of Aboriginal peoples.

Even though today there is an increasing inclusion and recognition of Aboriginal philosophies in academic circles, this alone does not characterize these systems as distinctly or predominantly philosophical. Philosophical thought has been at the heart of Aboriginal societies since time immemorial. There have always been philosophers amongst the people. In fact, they have a tradition of intellectuals called the Chinshinabe, the Elders and traditional Teachers who are the caretakers of cultural and sacred knowledge. They take on the responsibility of maintaining the flow of Nebwakawin (wisdom) that passes from generation to generation.

In particular, I am concerned with the axiological aspects of this philosophical system; in other words, values, ethics and to a lesser extent, aesthetics. Concerning Aboriginal philosophy as a whole, it is, I believe, important that I indicate some of the central foundational ideas of this system so that there is a general context to work from with regard to the content of this work. I do not mean to suggest that it is possible to summarize all aspects of Aboriginal metaphysics, ontology, epistemology, etc. into a few sentences, but there are some key philosophical tenets that must be expressed so that this work can have contextual integrity.

A belief in Manitou is fundamental to Aboriginal philosophy. Existence is Creation and the Creation Story sets out the process and purpose of this physical reality. In Basil Johnston's (Odawa) words:

> Because Manitou is a being existing in the supernatural sphere, this spirit is super-ordinate to human experience, knowledge and description. But it is taken for granted and accepted as true that Kitchi-Manitou created the universe, the world and the beings upon, above, and below, both corporeal and incorporeal, from a vision or dream. Creation, by which the mystical vision was brought into the realm of physical reality, is seen as an act of generosity and a sharing of the Manitou's goods with those in need.

Aboriginal philosophy was received in original instructions from Manitou, with the intent to guide people through life.

Aboriginal philosophy is a philosophy of interconnection. Creation is understood as both the source and unity in movement of all life. This holistic perspective is at the very heart of my system of inquiry and explanation. It aims to isolate and explain some of the philosophical aspects of this system, despite the recognition that such divisions are artificial to the perceived understanding of the Aboriginal Philosophy.

There are detailed oral Teachings about all these subjects, and the skin of an onion metaphorically symbolizes them. When we look at the onion we see it as a whole; but, in fact, we are only looking at the surface. If we remove this skin we find another layer deeper down. Remove this one and another is below, and so on. Aboriginal philosophy is very much like the onion. The more one learns the more one finds, and the process continues, going deeper and deeper, all through one's life.

Aboriginal tradition already has an educational method as part of its structure. In traditional and contemporary times the Elders and the traditional Teachers are the ones who guide the apprentice on his or her path of learning since the education of an Aboriginal person happens throughout the lived-experience of that person. Joseph Couture (Cree/Métis) explains this when he states:

> The doing that characterizes the Aboriginal Way is a doing that concerns itself with being and becoming a unique person, one fully responsible for one's own life and actions within family and community. Finding one's path and following it is a characteristic Aboriginal enterprise that leads to or makes for the attainment of inner and outer balance.

The major difference between Aboriginal views of the physical world and Western science lies in the premise accepted by Aboriginals and rejected by scientists: the world in which we live is alive. Many scientists believe this idea to be primitive superstition and consequently the scientific explanation rejects any nuance of interpretation that would credit the existence of activities as having partial intelligence or sentience. American Aboriginals look at events to determine the spiritual activity supporting or undergirding them. Science insists, albeit at a great price in understanding, that the observer be as detached as possible from the event he or she is observing. Aboriginals thus obtain information from birds, animals, rivers, and mountains that is inaccessible to modern science. Aboriginals also know that human beings must participate in events, not isolate themselves from occurrences in the physical world.

For a Western-educated audience the notion of a tree with spirit is a difficult concept to grasp...[i.e.,] the universe is alive. Therefore, to see an Aboriginal speaking with a tree should not carry the message of mental instability; on the contrary, this is a scientist engaged in research!

This Primary Experiential Knowledge method strives to achieve exactly this kind of research: metaphysical certainty through already existing structures of Aboriginal metaphysics, ontology, axiology and epistemology. It is, as Couture (Cree/Métis) notes:

> ...a question of discovering through direct experience that there are entities on other planes, entities which are not of the realm of illusion, or hallucination. It is learning to become quiet, "attentive" as Black Elk says. It is a question of entering into Aboriginal psychic areas, and of learning to live by Aboriginal rules of time and space, such rules are none other than universal, cosmic or "natural" laws.

When I explain the role of insights and knowledge from a spiritual source, I am, of course, assuming that that spiritual realm is real and approachable. My understanding of Creation and Manitou is one that speaks of the absolute oneness of reality. Indeed, I am speaking of absolute truths and an absolute reality. Traditional Teachings and traditional Teachers have been quite clear on this point, and through the development and growth of my Primary Experiential Knowledge, I not only believe, but also know with certainty that the truth, as evident in the way of the action of Creation, is absolute. I share this view with others who follow the traditional protocols. These are not exactly the usual words and sentiments of an old academic philosophy major, but this does bring us to one of the fundamental problems of discussing the appropriateness and validity of my approach: academia's apprehension of absolutes.

We are witness to a unique time when the old is becoming new; we are rediscovering the underlying texture of other Aboriginal philosophies. It is my hope that my people never lose a sense of their worldview and that indeed others will begin to appreciate the insights that we can bring to the truth of the universe.

WORLDVIEW OF THE CLIENT
E. Spinelli (Age: 55)
Therapist & Educator– London, England

The meaning of pain defines suffering. So anyone dealing with hurting people must at the outset be mindful of the constructed world in which these people live. To impose any other world upon them is to show disrespect to the person and to devalue them and their experience/defining process as a person. Indeed, since we as human beings can rarely alleviate all suffering it is our job to help people find the meaning in pain and suffering and thereby survive and even thrive within this life. If we consider the analogy of an athlete, he/she may expect and even embrace pain during a game but may suffer if his/her injury disables him/her or causes his/her team to lose. A person who is injured intentionally and ignored is likely to suffer more than one who is hurt accidentally and treated with care.

Suffering is a central concern of psychotherapy. In addition to helping patients acknowledge and bear pain, therapists use a variety of approaches to help them put pain into perspective. (1) For example, a therapist may explore whether the expectations of a patient disappointed by a friend are realistic, and if not, what reasons he/she may have for holding onto those expectations. Together they may uncover the patient's maladaptive schemas for interpreting reality or (2) use cognitive strategies to correct distorting tendencies such as a tendency to see life through the dark glasses of depression. (3) Therapists also recruit placebo or transference effects to shape the meaning of pain for patients of their healing interventions.

The task of putting profound suffering into perspective can require grappling with larger questions. For example, serious physical illness often prompts individuals to reassess what gives their lives significance. Survivors of childhood sexual abuse may need to rebuild their shattered assumptive worlds so as to achieve a new take on themselves, on their hopes, and on reality.

The father of psychotherapy, Sigmund Freud, identified the possession of a worldview as one of the ideal wishes of human beings. Although his friends and long-time correspondents Oscar Pfisterand and Romain Rolland tried to persuade him that religious and mystical experiences could not be understood in only scientific terms, Freud maintained his position that a scientific outlook and a religious worldview were mutually incompatible.

A person's Worldview helps to shape the meaning of his/her painful experience. An individual who trusts in God as a protector of good people may feel cheated, if not punished, by a diagnosis of cancer. A believer with a different understanding of God may wonder if the same illness is intended to discipline him/her or bring him/her closer. Cancer may remind a Buddhist of the need to transcend desire and attachment, an atheist of his/her most important accomplishments or values.

In treating a patient (and caring for them as a person) who is struggling with the larger meaning of pain or loss, therapists do well to identify the resources for dealing with suffering that are contained in his/her particular Worldview. Jews can find in the Psalms and in the story of Job precedent for the sufferer to call out to and question God. Christians can also see in Christ's suffering evidence that God cares about their suffering because he has taken it on himself—thus dignifying suffering on behalf of others. Buddhists find in the dharma support for detaching from the desire that leads to suffering. Atheists faced with suffering may instead take pride in their own integrity, intellectual honesty, or stoicism. A therapist may also need to help a patient address the particular challenges presented by his/her Worldview in coming to terms with suffering.

Individuals with a spiritual or theistic worldview often feel that someone cares about their pain and that they are not ultimately alone. However, they may also be struggling with the concept that a God who is powerful enough to have spared them illness did not choose to do so. Theological, philosophical, and popular texts that address this problem of theodicy include Rabbi Kushner's *When Bad Things Happen to Good People* and C. S. Lewis's *The Problem of Pain*. Rather than being expected to offer such philosophical consultations, clinicians will usually find that believing patients (not unlike nonbelievers) instead most often want a chance to be heard and to talk about their concerns with someone who will understand the importance those concerns have for them—someone who will neither suggest his own answers to their questions nor reduce them to something more psychodynamic. They may also need to reflect on, and to think through, their own beliefs and doubts. The account by the Christian apologist C. S. Lewis of his experience of his wife's death, *A Grief Observed*, is a compelling description of this process.

Therapists are sometimes inhibited in exploring a believer's struggle by a desire to stay close to the familiar role of discussing the psychological dimension of the patient's problems, or by a wish to respect the patient's privacy. This may cause them to underestimate their potential for helping patients disentangle the intertwined contributions of psychopathology, formative traumatic experiences, and/or patients' undeveloped understanding of the teachings of their own religious tradition.

A 42-year-old married Catholic mother worried that her diagnosis of ovarian cancer was a punishment from God for having had an abortion. Her view of God had not changed much since her time in Sunday School, and she seemed unaware that her fear did not accord with her church's teaching. On exploration, it appeared that these fears were also related to her growing up with a strict and punitive father, as well as to her tendency to respond to stress with worry and self-blame.

Treatment included reducing her initial extreme anxiety by using medication, then considering with her over several sessions the sources of her fears and most troubling beliefs. She and I explored her experiences of God and of prayer, and discussed the messages she received in Sunday school as compared with her developing adult understanding of forgiveness within her Catholic tradition. I also offered a referral to the in-hospital priest as a person who could better help her understand what her faith taught. Having achieved some perspective on the contribution of her beliefs to her anxiety, she was able to clarify and then to deepen her trust in God as she entered the terminal phase of illness.

As in this case, a patient's religious Worldview can appear to be adding to his/her suffering—for example, by inducing unreasonable guilt. Consultation with a colleague who shares, or is more familiar with, the nuances of the patient's faith tradition can be very useful in distinguishing what the tradition actually holds compared with the patient's own interpretation.

Working through issues such as these can often help prevent estrangement of believers from some of their more important relationships at a time when they need them most—with God, if the patient feels they are no longer on speaking terms, and from religious friends who may not be able to tolerate the patient's hard questions.

Individuals with a naturalistic or atheistic worldview consciously reject a purposeful explanation for the universe. As a result, they may feel ultimately alone and anxious in bearing pain. Like many sophisticated believers, they see illness as no one's fault except perhaps their own through mistakes they made in bringing it on or failing to detect it in its early forms. In contrast, however, they often struggle to achieve a kind of Eriksonian integrity, or ability to live and die consistent with who they are. Some of these individuals seek out a clinician's help to review their lives, consolidate their own commitments, and find a secular perspective that will integrate these core values.

An atheistic scientist with lung cancer came for treatment because of anxiety about dying and difficulty thinking through whether or not she should request assisted suicide. Growing up in a disadvantaged neighborhood, she had been befriended by a teacher and then gone on to become extremely successful as a "self-made" leader in her field. What helped her most with her anxiety was to realize (as she had the night before learned that she had been granted tenure) that she could live without her work, and that the scientific and personal integrity that had given her life value was a legacy that she could pass on to others.

Suffering makes many people realize that they are uncertain or ambivalent about their philosophy of life. They may consider themselves as "lapsed" churchgoers or skeptics who have rejected organized religion but retained a strong sense of personal spirituality. A number of challenges face therapists in attempting to help agnostic people clarify their beliefs about what matters most, think through their questions, and consolidate their values so as to live in accord with their deepest commitments. One such challenge is to determine when a therapist should be the one to help the person sort through the spiritual and emotional aspects of his struggle.

A 53-year-old poet/artist came for help in dealing with his terminal illness. He listed several problems: his wife's distress and talk of suicide if he died; rage at feeling he was at the mercy of "a film director who keeps you in the dark about your role in life;" sadness at losing "the poignant beauty of life;" and feelings of guilt (which he saw as irrational) involving the sense that his suffering might be a deserved punishment for being a negligent father and a poor citizen to the community. As an admirer of Freud's cold honesty, he was unable to believe that death was any kind of "going to the light," but he also described himself as engaged in an intense spiritual quest, reading everything he could find about how to face it with some kind of solace and peace.

It became clear that he could not easily accept the narcissistic injury that death represented, but neither could he believe that "the exquisite beauty of a butterfly's wing came about by accident." He had not been religious since his Bar Mitzvah, but his Jewishness was somehow central to his spiritual quest.

What he wanted from a professional was primarily an admiring, attentive-enough audience and reassurance that he was on the right track in sorting out the various influences throughout his life on his attitudes, his values, and his hopes for himself and his family. He was ambivalent about whether he needed ongoing psychotherapy.

In the process of a consultation, he eventually came to feel that he was already actively engaged in the work of dying—that is, of bringing together these aspects of himself and of taking into account the psychological influences without letting them determine his responses. For example, reflecting on how he had reconciled with his father, he could see the potential for reconciling the sharply conflicting parts of himself and for helping his wife find a way to go on. To put it another way, he was on his way to forging out of painful experience his own perspective, not just on his current illness, but on life, and on himself as someone who had lived through many losses before. The challenge for the therapist in consulting with this highly imaginative and articulate man was how to facilitate, support, and acknowledge the connections he was making between his suffering and his beliefs, without getting in his way by delving into either psychological or spiritual aspects of the man's struggle on his own initiative.

Suffering people need to feel that their therapists not only take seriously their search for answers to ultimate questions such as the meaning of their suffering, but that they are willing to join them in this search. We must always remember that our experience is one that is constructed and we all need allies to walk with us in this journey of constructing the world within which we live.

WORLDVIEW OF THE ABSOLUTE
C. Shiva Krishna (Age: 64)
Brahman Priest/Philosopher/Guru/Educator
Bangladesh & India

I am a man who was born to the highest level of Indian culture, trained as a priest, a philosopher and an educator. I have seen much in life and have a story to tell about how we may apprehend the true universe of Brahma.

If we begin with the basic story of the Atom we can follow the commonsense perception that makes one believe that the ultimate stuff of the world is matter. The senses give us the intimations of the existence of physical bodies outside our own. We, generally speaking, live in a world presented by the senses, and the senses happen to come in contact only with material bodies, for they are gross even as matter is.

In the beginning, human attempts to understand the nature of the world ended in the discovery that some physical element must be the reality. Some thought that water was the primal substance. Certain others felt it was fire, some air, and so on. This is the natural consequence of the most primitive form of perception. Matter was taken to be what it was observed to be. There are the five gross elements, and everything seems to be composed of them. Some ancient speculators, no doubt, felt a need to accept the presence of a mind, in addition to these elements, but its position in the scheme of things was so weak that it was superseded by the feeling that the elements are, somehow, the ultimate realities of the world.

But this state of affairs could not continue for long. Matter became one of the two realities making up the world, the other being mind or thought. Matter is mere extension—the material of all bodies, animal and human alike, though the human being has a thinking and understanding faculty, thus distinguishing him from the lower animals which are said to be, more or less, automatons moved by instinct. There were also others to whom matter appeared as the symbol of imperfection, the dark "quality-less" basis of the world, and could be designated as non-being. Only the mind contemplating it could be real.

These thinkers took little interest in the constitution of matter, for, to them, it had little significance in the realm of realities. Matter was also believed to be the potential state of what is more real, the latency of the form, a stage in the process of development. The world of matter was held to be not a static being, but a movement, a march towards the actualization of pure form. Matter, again, was thought to consist of sleeping centers of energy or force. Minds are such centers risen to consciousness, while matter is their un-evolved state. Others felt that matter is an attribute of reality that appears as matter from one viewpoint and as thought from another.

It is interesting to note that present-day science has slowly risen from the perception of solid matter by a gradual improvement of the instruments of its knowledge. The world which was supposed to be consisting of the gross elements and various kinds of objects was reduced to a few simple chemical elements which were thought to be incapable of further simplification. But these elements were again analyzed, and, with Dalton, came the theory that these consisted of minute granular substances or atoms. The number of the atoms was supposed to correspond to that of the chemical elements, of which the former are the constituents. But then came, again, the wonderful research of a group of eminent pioneers of a revolution in science, which revealed the electrical nature of the atom and the possibility of breaking it into further minute elements. The cause of the difference in the various kinds of atoms was found to be something startlingly new. The difference was discovered to be not in the quality of the constituents of the atom, but in their number, arrangement and manner of movement. The constituents themselves are identical in nature in all the atoms of the different chemical elements. The atoms are made up of positive and negative charges of electricity, called protons and electrons. Later, several other phases, such as neutrons that have no charges in them, and positrons, which are positive electrons, were discovered. The atom is now described as something similar to a solar system. The central nucleus of the atom is comparable to the sun, with the electrons revolving round it as the planets. There is an immensity of space between these revolving particles and the central nucleus, as well as between the particles themselves. These electrical constituents of the atom are supposed to be the irreducible minimum reality in the world.

Scientists are as yet unable to determine the "smallest" piece of matter. The best that they are able to do is find an "electron cloud" that is not pure matter and yet functions in a dynamic way. As such the scientific community has not been able to come to the last element in the analysis of matter. They have reached only as far as dynamic relationships and their mysterious functions, and nothing else. Even the nature of these dynamic relationships is not known, only their behaviour is observed. One cannot say what electricity is, but only how it behaves. Electric energy is a name given to the farthest process discovered in the world by instruments available to the methods of science. Energy is not being but becoming, and its activity is the same as its existence. Modern physics has given a quietus to the age-old materialistic theory of the world, and has landed in the realm of a dynamic process of organisms acting symmetrically on one another. Being has given way to becoming. Science, however, has remained blind to the fact that even a process cannot be, unless it is observed by an intelligence. The highest reality cannot be any object, though it be a cosmic object, like energy, which is distinguished from the consciousness that knows it.

The error in the scientist's way of knowing comes into high relief when they face insurmountable difficulties in the search for reality. For them, electric energy and light appear to have the character of waves. All phenomena are now supposed to be a continuous process of particles. It is not difficult to note that isolated particles cannot form a process. And yet this appears, to the eye of the scientist, to be the juggling activity of the ultimate constituents of matter and light. He forgets that there are certain restricting conditions imposed upon his knowledge by the very nature of the instruments he uses in his researches as well as by the structure of his mind and sense-organs. One cannot know truth by remaining as an observer outside it, for the limitations on individual knowledge are removed only when the distinction between the knower and the known is abolished in a self-identical awareness.

The dilemma in which the scientist is landed by his defective means of knowing becomes clear from another problem raised in science that goes by the name of the Principle of Indeterminacy. This is the outcome of the inability of the scientific method of observation to fix the track of the movement of electrons in an atom. The laws of mechanics fail here, and the electron does not seem to obey any law known to man. It is seen to make jumps from one point of space to another in a manner that cannot be determined by any scientific law. This predicament has led many to think that there is no freedom in the universe, that there is no choice, and that indeterminacy reigns supreme everywhere. This conclusion is evidently exaggerated, for the principle only means that the ways of tracing the movements of the electron are not known to scientists yet, and that their present instruments of research are not as subtle as the force with which the electrons move. This cannot be taken to amount to a denial of the causal law and the system with which the universe appears to be governed.

The present trend of science has been towards an idealistic monism, affirming finally a mental or spiritual principle as the ultimate stuff of the universe. Newton's physics and Euclid's geometry have given rise to the theory of relativity and the geometry of the four-dimensional manifold. The mechanistic laws of Newtonian physics and the theorems and deductions of Euclid hold good in our world, with our space-time, but are proclaimed to be inapplicable to the inconceivably small realm of microphysics, as also to the inconceivably great universe envisaged in astrophysics. Modern physics gives, thus, not a material world in the old sense of the term, but a relative structure to be equated, in the end, with the functions of a cosmic mind or consciousness.

Behind the man of commonsense perception is the chemist. Behind chemist is physicist. Behind the physicist is the mathematician. Symbols and equations have taken the place of physical bodies. But these, however, are contained in the mind of the mathematician. And behind the activity of the mathematical mind is the searching analysis of the philosopher.

We create a division between the knower and the known because it suits our practical needs and conveniences. It is the nature of reality to appear in a duality of the seer and the seen when it is made the object of individual perception. The dualist hypothesis would give strong support to the pragmatist theory that the notion of reality is relative to human interest. We are born in a world of duality, and the very fibre of our make-up is saturated with a consciousness of its tremendous significance. We think in terms of duality, feel and act in accordance with it. It is natural, therefore, that truth, to us, should be relative to our dualistic interests. The pragmatist attitude is the immediate result of our attachment to sense perception. In its view, what is known is not the real as such, but our purposes objectified. We seem to abstract from the real what we need at the present state of our minds, and identify our needs with reality. We appear to be concerned with the meaning that things have for us in our day-to-day affairs, and not with the things themselves. The pragmatic method consoles us by returning to us our own desires in the form of truth, but not truth in itself. It is true that, for psychology, the subject is sharply distinguished from the object, but philosophy cannot be content with such a superficial attitude to knowledge. Psychology is concerned with mind and its behaviour on a dualistic basis, but it cannot validate the notion that there is a real distinction between the knower and the known, even if our surface-life may seem to demand it. An unquestioning clinging to the immediate sense-percepts is the cause of our blind belief in the ultimate division of things. There cannot be knowledge of truth or a correspondence between knowledge and fact if the object is outside the jurisdiction of consciousness.

The relation of matter to consciousness can be explained only if an organic intimacy of the one with the other is accepted. A completely detached object cannot become a content of consciousness. The mind cannot know even the existence of matter if they are ultimately different from each other. There can be relation between two terms only when they possess some qualities at least common to both. Matter and consciousness are, to the dualist, elements which are supposed to possess characters that have no relation of similarity. But, then, the existence of the object cannot become a content of the mind. Man cannot know that there is a world outside if it is true that he is not a member in its constitution. Knowledge-relation always presupposes a third element, which makes the connection between the subject and the object possible. Entities possessing dissimilar natures cannot come in contact with, or even know the presence of, each other. The acceptance of a principle relating the subject and the object in perception, and yet different from them both, takes us to the great truth of a consciousness that cannot be restricted by factors either external or internal. It appears to have an instantaneous existence, unconditioned, and at once timeless. When we accept such a principle, we come, perhaps, to the realisation of the highest end of all philosophical quests. Pure consciousness should naturally be omnipresent, omniscient and omnipotent. It gets identified with the ideal pointed out by the concept of God. God is the infinite. He is neither a knower nor a known, but a transcendent being.

The consciousness of imperfection implies the possibility of perfection. To recognize the finitude of oneself is to step at once into the realm of the infinite. When finitude is known, the fact of the contingency of the knower's transcending it is implied in it. The finite has no significance except in contradistinction to the infinite. The moral argument based on the aspirations of man points to a reality in which they can be fulfilled. There is an urge in everyone to break the boundaries of imperfection and reach out to an unlimited existence, wherein is a promise of the satisfaction of all the sides of one's nature. Man is never contented with anything that he possesses, for he feels, in spite of his possessions, an inherent sense of a serious lack of something which does not seem to be included in anything that he is blessed with in this world. Even the rulership over all things will leave behind a want of something higher and a yearning to obtain one knows not what. There is a longing for eternal life, for boundless knowledge, for unrestricted happiness, for light, freedom and immortality. This restless aspiration refuses to be cajoled by the poor presentation of earthly glory. The world seems to be busy, changing and moving, adjusting and adapting itself to conditions beyond itself, pointing to the weird vision of some wondrous essence at which it is aiming as its long desired destination.

Union and separation, birth and death, struggle and aspiration, do not have any significance unless they imply a being that is beyond change and transformation. The contingent character of things seems to oppose one state of finitude to another, suggesting a self-expansion of the finite in an experience wider than its own, in which it includes the properties of the other finites, and by which it overcomes the lower oppositions in a higher harmony. Every perception is an ardent effort to attain a greater unity, in which the essences of all percepts are transmuted and absorbed. All created elements tend to find their solace in a fulfillment of their nature by an attempt to overcome all cramping situations that stand in the way of such development. The relational character of finite objects is determined by the action of other finite objects on them, which fact leads us to the discovery of the universe being an organism presided over by a supreme Intelligence. The existence of the finite as the finite is dependent on the conditions determining finitude as a whole, and so it has to rise from its lower conditioned state to more and more inclusive ones that reveal greater and greater coherence and harmony. **Therefore our life in the world can be accounted for only by the existence of the Absolute and the absolute can be reduced to relationships.**

WORLDVIEW OF THE SCIENTIST
Sigmund Freud (Age: 60)
The Ignorance of Science

I wish to share with you a particularly German notion known as Weltanschauung. The term has no good translation into English but in essence it means an intellectual construction that gives a unified solution of all the problems of our existence in virtue of a comprehensive hypothesis. It is a way of viewing the world and making sense out of the world.

While as a psychoanalyst I am concerned about the Weltanschauung of people, the science of studying the human mind is itself quite unsuited for constructing its own Weltanschauung. As a scientist, however, I can confidently state that psychoanalysis is able to buy into the scientific Weltanschauung that guides us in our scientific pursuits. That is, we have a unified explanation of nature and the universe that claims that the only source of knowledge is the intellectual manipulation of variables that give carefully verified observations.

Of course there are always those who contend that such a Weltanschauung is both empty and unsatisfying, that it overlooks all the demands for meaning that humanity places upon itself. I cannot disagree with this claim, but at the same time, I study the human animal the same way the scientist studies the atom and I cannot neglect the scientific principles that guide me. The difference...is that my study must take into account the distinction between emotional motivation and true knowledge when understanding the human mind.

What I am saying is that there is a great deal of difference between what we believe in the systems of religion and what is "real" "factual" knowledge. We must never confuse the two, for to think the one is as valid as the other is to be greatly misled. We must always make use of our critical powers in the task of separating our beliefs and our knowledge, for otherwise we will be overwhelmed with narrow prejudices that make us nothing more than religious fanatics or political radicals.

I realize that there is a great deal that we do not know, but what I do know is that Weltanschauung is central to nature of psychoanalysis. However, psychoanalysis is not, in my opinion, in a position to "create" a Weltanschauung of its own. It has no need to do so, for it is a branch of science and can subscribe to the scientific Weltanschauung (as long as that view is not corrupted by scientific myths of its own making). Of course, a scientific Weltanschauung is not deserving of such a high-sounding name, for it does not take everything into its scope, but rather, is incomplete and makes no claim to be comprehensive (at least not in its proper form). Scientific thought is still a crying infant.

A Weltanschauung based upon science has, apart from the emphasis it lays upon the real world, essentially negative characteristics, such as that it limits itself to truth and rejects illusions. Those of us who are dissatisfied with this state of things and who desire something more for their momentary peace of mind may look for it where they can find it and I wish them no ill. However, we cannot do any other in our pursuit of truth than admit our utter ignorance and seek to take a systematic account of the reality around us.

WORLDVIEW OF THE UNFEELING
Len Eggose (Age: 27)

My worldview has changed greatly over the years. Growing up in a small hamlet on the Canadian prairies, the world did not extend far past my father's fields. Over the years, however, I have traveled much and met many fascinating people that have forced me to shift my thinking. I think of my neighbours in Chicago, Illinois that struggled to make a living. I think of my neighbours in Palm Desert, California who struggled only to improve their golf game. I remember my "house-mother" at my rooming house in Johannesburg, South Africa, who ran a hostel from her childhood home, inherited after her parents died of AIDs. I think of how I sat in worship in SOWETO, starring up at the ceiling of the church, looking through the bullet holes through to the sky above. I think of the people I have sat with as a counselor or pastoral companion, many of whom that have taken their last breath as I sat with them. Yet, none of these experiences have changed my worldview as much as a chance encounter in a massive crowd of people in a third world city.

Being a tall man standing in a crowd I felt people pushing this way and that, but had little sense of the people (other than the tops of their heads). Then suddenly I noticed someone tugging on my arm. Casting a quick glance, what I saw shocked me. Hanging on my forearm was a small, frail woman, bent over, leaning partially on a mean thin crutch crudely constructed out of twigs. Her feet were swollen, barefoot, and she had no toes. As I let out a gasp of revulsion and stepped back, she lost her balance and fell towards me. As I caught her, I noticed how thin and weak she really was. My eyes shifted, tracing the length of her arm to where her hands should have been, finding only dark, dirty fingerless stumps. Lifting my eyes to hers, asking if she was "O.K." the breath was again torn from my chest. Her right eye hung from a gouged temple, dry, dead and staring coldly to one side, while her left eye danced upwards to meet mine, and then dropped away at the sight of my horrified expression. Her thin cheeks wrinkling into an awkward smile of embarrassment, she slowly regained her balance and continued on her way.

It was clear that this woman suffered from leprosy. As the years have passed I cannot help but think back to that few seconds on a busy street. I cannot help but imagine how this disease, that slowly attacks the nerve cells of the body, must have slowly consumed her life. The gradual loss of the sense of pain must have been very subtle at first. Perhaps beginning with a simple sliver in her hand going undetected, then becoming infected and resulting in the loss of a hand or finger. Perhaps, as she was walking down the street, she stubbed a toe, resulting in a sprain or break that went unnoticed, eventually killing the limb. And then, as the nerves that trigger the eyelid to blink every few seconds for lubricating moisture became affected, her right eye began to dry out, becoming blind and useless.

I have thought about the lessons that encounter can teach us; that to feel no pain when part of the body is hurt is a dangerous thing. For the church, to lose the capacity to feel pain will only result in a church that is crippled, weak and blind.

WORLDVIEW OF THE FORGIVEN
The Terrorist

The din of excited reporters jostling along the edge of the fence was more reminiscent of a schoolyard than a military installation. Echoes of questions filled the air as reporters searched for a quote or defiant phrase. Yet, the man did not move, kneeling silently upon the burning hot sand. Only the armed guards looming like sinister rostrum statues along the rail kept the media mob at bay.

"The people have the right to know!" shouted a reporter.

"All questions about the capture of this notorious terrorist will be answered in due time!" countered the commander as he stepped towards the fence.

"Give us something to report!" cried another frustrated journalist.

Slowly, deliberately, the commander stepped forward, edging his weathered face so that only the fence and a few precious inches separated him from the row of anxious writers. "You want a quote?" The commander bit with his jagged martial accent.

"You want something to report to the people?"

Taking a half step back and standing to his full height, the commander raised his hand with a menacing point while lowering his voice to its most intimidating intonation.

"You tell the people of the world this: 'The REPUBLIC stands strong. The REPUBLIC will not be intimidated by any terrorist threat. And make no mistake—this terrorist murderer will pay for his crimes!"

Then, with military precision, the commander turned and strode the fifty paces to the figure kneeling in the sand. With a deliberate flick of his wrist the commander signalled for two soldiers to scoop the figure up and follow the commander into a tent.

The media paused until they were satisfied that no further information could be gleaned. Then, suddenly, the focus of the mob shifted as they set about spreading the news, "The Terrorist is captured!"

Later that day, with the soft scraping sounds of sand being dragged across a hard surface, the broken figure finally fell in a tumble of cloak and hair and skin.

"Get up you murderous scum," murmured the soldier who had tossed him to the floor of the cave. "Get back on your knees; this is your new home—until your execution."

Slowly the figure crawled back to a kneeling position, knowing full well that another beating was the penalty of non-compliance. Thankful though he was to no longer be blindfolded, the shackles on his wrists and ankles still bit deeply into his tendons. He could no longer move his fingers and he was sure that there was no life left in his feet. His back ached and his knees bled, but for the first time his eyes were able to scan his surroundings. It was a cave—a dark, cold, damp cell—but it beat the burning hot sand of the midday heat.

The darkness soon returned, however, as the soldier closed the door. The last sound the prisoner heard was the metal clicking of the latch. He was left there in the darkness and silence, kneeling. While he was thankful to be out of the heat of the sun, the dark coolness of the cell was not his friend for long.

After a few days, this thin, frail, unshaven man began to long for the heat of the day and the light of the sun. Curled up in the dark cell with no light there was no interrogation, no trial, no human contact. Smelly, dirty, hungry, thirsty, lonely and sore, he was reminded in every breath that his future held only one thing—punishment.

The man who had once stood proudly, publicly and defiantly against the world's powers was now bent low. He was forced to yield to the shackles about his hands and feet, and forced to lay in his own excrement because he lacked the strength to carry out his bodily duties with dignity. The once proud man now lay silent, contemplating his next public appearance, as a gruesome spectacle for the masses as the REPUBLIC exacted its revenge.

The next days (or at least what seemed like days to this man) were full of the same torturous thoughts. Then, out of the timeless depths of his internment, a striking sound broke the stillness. He heard marching on the stone pavement above, a steady rhythm that gave his starved senses something to fixate upon. It was a marching so steady and massive that it took many minutes to pass overhead. "It must be a parade," thought the prisoner. The happy thought of a festival and parade was instantly lost as a jolt of fear ricocheted through his body. Now, he realized, the end was near.

Still chained, the prisoner rolled upon the cold ground in tears, sobbing silently. He thought back to the days of his youth, and how his father would hold him and whisper to him about the importance of his name.

"Remember, your name means, 'the son of the father,' so you never need worry, my son, your father will always be with you,"[2] His father would whisper in his ear.

Oh, how he missed his father, how he missed his family. The memories were swept away as he heard the crowd gathering above. He could hear the crowd calling his name. His mind raced, his heart beat uncontrollably. He knew how ugly a mob could get. Timorous, he lay upon the floor shaking, for he knew that his execution was to be a ghastly spectacle, and worst of all, he knew he deserved it.

The hollow sounds of marching came closer as a small detail of soldiers approached the door of his stone cell. They were coming for him. This was it; the marching stopped. He could hear the thin tin rattling of keys and the click of the latch. The cell flooded with light and his eyes winced at the shock, his head pounding with dread. In the midst of the smell, the refuse and the fear, a soldier stepped forward and grabbed the chains and silently unlocked the shackles. The terrorist fell back to the floor as the latches burst open, releasing his scabby wrists and ankles.

Slowly he took a breath, pulling his limbs underneath his body. He took over a minute to stand, and even then only tentatively, wavering before the soldier. It was there, in the midst of that new light from the door, that he realized just how thin, and weak, and dirty he had become. He was ashamed, for he saw himself as he truly was, a broken man who was soon to die.

Yet it was at that moment that he discovered the meaning of love, the meaning of grace, the meaning of compassion and most of all, the meaning of atonement. It was at that moment that this terrorist who had killed in the name of God finally understood the character of God. For as this broken man stood at the entrance of that cell he heard twelve words that changed his life: "Barabbas, the Republic has set you free. We will kill Jesus instead."

GLOSSARY

Key Terms:

Autopoeic: Derived from the Greek words *Auto* meaning "self" and *Poien* meaning, "to create." The term refers to the process of forming and defining oneself over/against the surrounding environment. This relating process includes how the individual relates to society and the environment.

Existo: A Latin term meaning, "I exist." The term carries the connotation of a state of being and through this state of being defining its location and meaning in relation to the rest of existence in an active and dynamic way.

Fons: A Latin term, meaning "the source."

Fons Vitae: A Latin term meaning the "source of life" or "existential source." ("vitae" is the genitive singular form of "life.") The term carries the connotation that every idea, notion and personal narrative (as well as personal existence) has a source that helps to define its purpose and relationship with the rest of existence.

Frontal Lobe: The region of the brain's cortex in front of the central fissure. This area is known as the rostral or symbolic region responsible for higher thinking.

Mortalitas: A Latin term meaning, "death." The term carries with it the connotation of the end of being, limited existence (and in this book then the uniquely personal nature of human life.)

Myth: A story (not necessarily a fictional or made up story). Generally, however, the story is seen as almost unbelievable unless one grew up in the culture where the story was perpetuated.

Mythopoeic: Derived from the Greek words *Mythos* meaning, "story" and *Poien* meaning, "to create." The term refers to the way in which larger stories and myths are incorporated and personalized to form individual life narratives. This "myth creating" is often the nature of the religious/faith life and is used by a person's psychological structure to organize relationships within the self and with the external world.

Noumena: A term that is meant to describe reality as it "actually is" in all of its depths of complexity. We as human beings will never fully grasp reality as it truly is.

Ontological: The study of the essence of things; the study of the nature and essence of being.

Opus: A Latin term meaning, "work."

Opus Vitae: A Latin term that means literally one's life work. The overall connotation is of being creative and constructive in the way one spends his/her energy. It is defining to one's existence because it is actually how one expresses his/her "being in the world."

Vita/Vitae: A Latin term that is best expressed as "existence" or "life".

Weltanschauung: A German term used in 17th to 19th century philosophy. The term refers to the notion of a "worldview" (an intuitive way of understanding the world).

POST-SCRIPT
A Theological Reflection

FONS VITAE

God fashioned the original humans as the icon of the divine, in the likeness of God (Gen 1:26-30).

Reflect upon these questions and then we will take some time to explore them:
1. What does the "image of God" mean?
2. In what way are we humans different from the rest of creation, and in what way are we like God?
3. How has sin affected the image?
4. Is this image relevant to how we define ourselves and to our growth?

A Reflection of God

The image of God may partially refer to intellectual and relational abilities that allow us to care for and rule over the earth. Our abilities to think and reason have clearly set us apart from the rest of creation (as the earth now suffers under our abuse and subjugation of it). However, our ability has been corrupted by sin (hence our abuse of creation instead of care for it), but humans still have the potential for much more.

Humans were made in the "image" and "likeness" of God (Gen 1:26). Other terms to describe the Hebrew notion here are: icon, representation, reflection and illustration. This is the one thing that distinguishes us from the animals. Beyond this one fact we are nothing more than complicated mud (like the animals who were not made in God's image.)

> *God made mud.*
> *God got lonesome.*
> *So God said to some of the mud, "Sit up!"*
> *"See all I've made," said God, "the hills, the sea, the sky, the stars."*
> *And I was some of the mud that got to sit up and look around.*
> *Lucky me. Lucky mud.*
> *I, mud, sat up and saw what a nice job God had done.*
> *Nice going, God.*

> *Nobody but you could have done it, God! I certainly couldn't have.*
> *I feel very unimportant compared to You.*
> *The only way I can feel the least bit important is to think of all the mud*
> *that didn't even get to sit up and look around.*
> *I got so much, and most mud got so little.*
> *Thank you for the honour!*
> *Now mud lies down again and goes to sleep.*
> *What memories for mud to have!*
> *What interesting other kinds of sitting-up mud I met!*
> *I loved everything I saw!*
> *Good night.*
>
> ~Anonymous

There is no doubt that we are unique. Whatever our affinities with the animal realm, we are drastically distinguished from all other earthly creatures by the fact that we alone have been created in the divine image and are intended by disposition to be a *"godly creature."*

Although humans were created to be "God-like" (if only in the caretaker function), we are now sinful, and unlike God, we are neither righteous, moral or faithful (Rom. 3:10, 23). Nevertheless, we are still considered to be in God's image (Gen 9:6; Jam. 3:9), so while the image is tarnished, something of what we were intended for does remain.

1. One possibility is that we still have the unique capacity (intellectually) to care for the earth (as defined by our creation mandate). However this capacity has been twisted so that we now subjugate and abuse creation for our own selfish ends and desires.

2. Thomas Aquinas located the image in the human ability to think and reason, to use language and art, far surpassing the abilities of any animals.

3. A "widely accepted interpretation" is that the "image" is our ability to make moral decisions which involve self-awareness and social awareness.

4. Emil Brunner says that it is our ability to have a relationship with God, reflected in the tendency of all societies to have forms of worship.

These four options are of course inter-related. Our relational abilities are the way in which we define our existence and the overall health of the created order. Our intellectual abilities are what gives our relational abilities power. In the end, however, it is our relationship with God that guides the morality that informs us whether we are using dominion rightly, and whether our relationships with God and humans are right.

Rationality and dominion help distinguish humans from animals, so they may be considered aspects of the image of God, but they do not constitute all that the image is. Rather, it is the purpose for which we use rationality and dominion that is of greater importance. People who have low intelligence and limited dominion are, if they love, closer to the desired image of God than a wicked genius dictator is. Mental skills and ruler-ship are God-like only if they are used in a moral way. Aquinas' emphasis on mental abilities is too broad, and the focus on dominion is too narrow. Humans are not unique in ruling, and we conform to the image of Christ primarily by serving and caring for others, not by ruling. The manner of our rule is far more important than the fact of our rule—it is essential that we rule morally, in right relationship with God and other beings.

Therefore, in a sense morality is entirely relational (how we relate with ourselves and the rest of creation). It involves our relationships with other people, and also with the divine Person, but it is the nature of the relationship, as much as the fact of it, that is important.

As we have already discussed throughout this book, each leg in the tripod of meaning connects with each other. This is, of course, so very true with our source. In particular, we are reminded that Christianity is an eschatological religion, meaning that in its narrative it points to an end-point when all the "brokenness" of life is fixed (and this means our clear untarnished image of God is restored). What will this look like, and how do we have a sense of what it was that we were intended to be like in the first place? In a word…"Jesus."

Jesus the Christ is the perfect image of God. As we are re-created in his image, by his presence in us we are being changed primarily in our morality, in our relationships with other humans and with God. Yet while the final change to restoration is so certain as to be talked about as a present fact (we have proof because of Jesus' physical resurrection), it is nevertheless nothing we will see fully in this lifetime. The best we can hope for is fleeting glimmers of love ("Now we see dimly, as in a dirty mirror," St. Paul says, *speaking about love*, "…then we shall know fully.")

Ever since the *Fall*, humans have been corrupt morally. They are not like God in their morality, but yet they are still considered to be in God's image (Gen 9:6; Jam 3:9). We are still called to live rightly and therefore morally. Humans still have vestiges of moral potential (though of course this is all relative, for even our best efforts are sinful in God's sight). Even the natural human has a potential for relative morality as all societies have some concept of right and wrong (as Paul mentions in Romans 2:15).

Jesus the Christ is the perfect image of God (2 Cor 4:4; Col 1:15; Heb 1:3), therefore all reading of scripture, all interpretation about how we live, act and conduct ourselves (even in judging others) must be through the prism of what Jesus has revealed in his actions. It is at this point where the *fons* breaks into the *opus*, for we are people saved by God's grace—this is our status—so we ought to strive to live in accordance with this status. We are to live as Christians by conforming to his likeness (2 Cor 3:18; Gal 4:19; Eph 4:13; Col 3:10). Jesus the Christ already sums up all that humanity is to be for he is a perfect representation of God to man; he is our perfect example. This life then is meant to be a process of slowly moving closer to the ideal. He is being formed in us and we are being conformed to his image. If we share in his humble estate in this life, we will share in his glory in the next age (Rom 8:29-30; 1 Cor 15:49; 1 John 3:2), existing more fully in his image.

Karl Barth, noting that God is trinity and relational and that humans are male and female, argued that relationship is at least part the divine image. It is clear that interpersonal relationships are important, for they are the sphere in which we are defined and our choices are manifested. They are also a prominent part of Jesus' teaching and one of the ways in which we must become more Christ-like. Jesus advocated emotions such as love (an interpersonal attitude) and faith (an interaction with God).

The church then should be an expression of these relationships (in their right form). We should assist with the needs of every aspect of creation. In particular we should be in the business of serving the image of God in humanity: providing for the physical needs, knowledge and emotional needs, and relational needs in society and with God.

Ephesians 4:12-13 summarizes some basic functions of the church—preparing God's people for works of service, and working toward unity in faith and the knowledge of Christ and maturity in him. Physical service, education, social needs and worship are all within the responsibility of the church.

Physical needs are important. Just as all humans have the duty to avoid bodily harm and cursing because of the image of God (Gen 9:6; Jam 3:9), Christians have the duty to take positive actions for others. The church not only teaches Christians to perform physical works of service that help the needy (Matt 25:31-46; Gal 6:10), it also sets an example of ministering to physical needs, as Jesus did. The church teaches social responsibility and morality to all who are being transformed into the image of Christ. It is often our failures in social areas that help us realize that our relationship with God is in need of repair.

The church preaches a message of reconciliation with God, which is a result of faith in Christ as Saviour.

Christianity interrelates all aspects of humanity—worship, social obligations, rational decisions, and physical assistance. The church teaches relationship with God, faith in him, love for him, holy living (Jam 1:27; Heb

5:14; 1 Jo 3:1-3; 5:2), and love for other humans, a love that leads to practical service (Heb 10:25). The church teaches the proper use of dominion, rationality, creativity, and personality.

In order for life to be set in a meaningful direction, we must first begin with a recognition of what we were created to be, why we have not achieved this, and what example we can use as a compass. We are made in God's image, but the potential value of this image (in this life) will not be realized unless we become conformed to the image of Christ in our relating to others and ourselves. To be living in God's image, we must be in a right relationship with God, creation and with other humans, using our minds and our authority to serve God, creation and our fellow humans. This is what it means to be in the image of God and conformed to the perfect image, his Son. Yet in the end, this is only achieved as a free gift of God.

OPUS VITAE

In the simplest of terms, the work-based meaning of life is "*To Serve God.*" Of course, this is really not as easy as it may sound, seeing as: 1) God does not need anything, and 2) We are corrupt creatures from the theological perspective and even our best action is lacking in the sight of a perfect God. As scriptures make clear, the only real life is in being in Christ, yet we will not experience the fullness of this life until the promised resurrection (that Jesus' bodily resurrection proved will be real for us) and our eternal purpose consists of living to the glory of God. Ultimately, it's the only thing that is truly worth anything in this world because it is only that relationship that survives the grave. It is only that resurrection promise and relationship that is infinitely substantive and that lasts forever! This is why I am such a proponent of hope in God's grace and theology in general. With the promise of the resurrection there is recognition of a hope. To reject the resurrection is to live in veiled emptiness. Veiled is the reality that no matter what you do, or how you succeed, or what wealth that you accumulate, it is somehow all in vain and un-fulfilling. Such is the core of the unauthentic life of work that we can choose to deceive ourselves and deny this fact. As the ancient lesson in the wisdom of the Preacher/King teaches.

> *"I gazed on all the works that my hands had achieved, and on the labour that I had laboured to do and succeed: and behold, all was arrogance and futility and annoyance to my mind, for in the end there was no profit under the sun.*
> *"All is vanity! We can spend our entire lives building and doing for ourselves, but ultimately, in the final analysis, there is no lasting profit for our success in this world. What meaning has it? It is all temporal.*

> *When we die and the bones are dried up, a few years pass, we are forgotten and our labours given to others, or turned to dust."*
> ~ECCLESIASTES 2:11, AUTHOR'S PARAPHRASE

The New Testament also makes clear the fact:

> *"According to my earnest expectation and my hope, that in nothing I shall be ashamed, but that with all boldness, as always, so now also Christ shall be magnified in my body, whether it be by life, or by death. For to me to live is Christ, and to die is gain."*
> ~PHILIPPIANS 1:20-21

The logic is clear, because all that we do in this life will eventually disappear and become nothing. Yet the relationship we have with our loving God makes our life in Christ the only lasting and therefore meaningful experience in life. The real meaning of a life in Christ is that we work to care for the creation that we were meant to care for. We are to be motivated by a love that is both an attitude and an action. The meaning emerges from the interrelationship between the works (done in love), and our relationship with God.

> *"Let us hear the conclusion of the whole matter: fear God, and keep His commandments; For this is the whole duty of humanity."*
> ~ECCLESIASTES 12:13

This is the "whole" of humanity! The purpose of humanity is to glorify God faithfully in reverential fear and obedience in servitude. In doing this, all good works in this life will follow naturally i.e., we will take care of our family, we will share the good news of God's free love with others, we will love others as ourselves and praise and glorify God. The meaning of Life is summed up in this! As Ecclesiastes says, it is the whole (complete purpose) of humanity. It is the Love of God wherein we will fear Him, keep his commandments, and therefore do the good works (remembering the better way of being motivated by love).

> *"By this we know that we love the children of God, when we love God, and keep his commandments. For this is the love of God, that we keep his commandments: and his commandments are not grievous."*
> ~1 JOHN 5:2-3

> *"Let us love one another... If we do not love, we do not know God."*
> ~1 JOHN 4:7-8

In this our lives are given meaning—the Greatest Commandment, Love the Lord Thy God! This love is shown by serving God in serving others in love. Even though this is probably not the answer that many who ask this question are seeking, it is the only answer which God gives. The love of God (and thus a love of God's Word) is paramount in this life.

So often people misconstrue that life is in food and drink, or that it is in the pleasures of this world. But these things are of the temporal, which in the end are worthless. The meaning of life is not in feeling good, it's not in amassing possessions, in worldly politics, power, or vain glory—it's in serving God so that His Kingdom (*not our own*) will be advanced. This is our life's work that will last forever because the fruits of that labour last forever. This is the Love of God, and the first commandment.

> *"Jesus said unto him. Thou shalt Love the Lord God with all thy heart, and with all thy soul, and with all thy mind. this is the first and Great commandment, and the second is like unto it, thou shalt love thy neighbour as thyself. On these two commandments hang all the law and the prophets."*
>
> ~MATTHEW 22:37-40

This is consistent with what we would expect. If we love God we will keep attempting to follow his instruction for life. Our opus, then, is to love God and therefore love our neighbour as ourselves (though we are sinful and will never really succeed at this...so we must be gracious with ourselves and others), and the Power wherein we were given to be witnesses will manifest itself in our spreading the gospel message to our neighbors. The greatest desire we have for ourselves is the kingdom of Heaven. And so (*loving our neighbour as ourselves*), we desire the same for them! For this cause we do feed the hungry, give the cup to those who thirst, clothe the naked and heal the sick. We also share the hope we have and the meaning to be found in life by bringing the good news of the gospel.

On these two commandments hang all the other commandments. In other words, if we love God, and love our neighbour as ourselves, we will keep all the other commandments for they hang on these (but we must lie to ourselves by believing that we will do it this side of the grave). In the great Westminster confession the question is posed, "What is the Chief end of man?" The answer is, "To Glorify God!" This is the meaning or purpose of life! It is not in serving ourselves or feeling sorry for ourselves when things don't go well. We weren't put here so that we could lounge in the lap of luxury and self indulgence and then die. We were put here to serve God and then to live. Obey, Love God, and keep His commandments. This is the whole of man (Ecc. 12:13).

> *"Love is reverence: it keeps its distance even as it draws near; it does not seek to absorb the other in the self or want to be absorbed by it; it rejoices in the otherness of the other..."*

*as reverence love is and seeks knowledge of the other,
not by way of curiosity nor for the sake of gaining power
but in rejoicing and in wonder."*

~H. RICHARD NIEBUHR

MORTALITAS

In the face of death stands the hope found in both eschatology and soteriology (the end-times and salvation). Therefore we have hope in Christ, or, more clearly, we have the assurance of a faithful God that the divine promise of forgiveness is true, the divine Father having even sent his Son to erase any doubt. This is despite our failings, our sinfulness and our utter ignorance of God. However, this does not deny the power and importance of death. No indeed. In fact, death makes the hope all that much greater, and the choices we make that much more powerful. Death frames and defines our entire existence, so as Dietrich Bonhoeffer stated it, *"Christ bids us, 'Come and die.'"*

While many existential philosophers contend that the human condition is bounded by death, the Christian emphasizes that when existence is in the hands of a loving God, there is always possibility and hope. Hence, the Christian view emphasizes futurity and possibility as the appropriate orientation for human life (though recognizing death as a defining form of life). Since our hope beyond death is based in the resurrection of Christ and our relationship found therein we can speak of our "hope in Christ."

With this relationship with the God who calls "Behold, I make all things new" (Revelation 21:5), we are opened up to a genuinely new historical experience where the temporal consideration of death is set aside. The God "with whom all things are possible" (Matthew 19:26), who "gives life to the dead and calls into existence the things that do not exist" (Romans 4:17) sets forth a new horizon with the hope of the resurrection. This hope of the resurrection calls us to become involved in the renewal of the world, and gives us courage to transform relationships and our relating to the world. A person with faith is transformed, and faith can expend itself in the pain of love and assume the form of a servant because it is upheld by the assurance of hope in the resurrection of the dead.

Christ calls us "Come and die." If you understand this, you will understand the importance of incorporating the hope of the resurrection of Christ into your life.

POST-SCRIPT: A Theological Reflection

Suffering is:
Not God's desire for us but occurs in the process of life.
Not given in order to teach us something, but through it we may learn.
Not given to punish us, but it is sometimes the consequence of sin.
Not given to us to teach others, but through it they may learn.
Not given because our faith is weak,
but through it our faith may be strengthened.
Not always to be avoided, but is sometimes chosen.
Both a destructive force, and a force that adds meaning to life.

~C. SIEGEL

REFERENCES

_____ (1998). Existential Wellness. *Ardell Wellness Report* 48:1.

Aagaard, J., Vestergaard, P., & Maarbjerg, K. (1988). Adherence to lithium prophylaxis: II. Multivariate analysis of clinical, social, and psychosocial predictors of nonadherence. *Pharmacopsychiatry* 21:166–170.

Abbruzzese, M., Ferri, S., & Scarone, S. (1997). The selective breakdown of frontal functions in patients with obsessive-compulsive disorder and in patients with schizophrenia: A double dissociation experimental finding. *Neuropsychologia* 35:907–912.

Abram, K., & Teplin, L. (1991). Co-occurring disorders among mentally ill jail detainees: Implications for public policy. *American Psychologist* 46:1036–1046.

Adams, D. (1995). *The restaurant at the end of the universe.* New York: Ballantine.

Adams, W. (1999). The interpretation of self and world: Empirical research, existential phenomenology and transpersonal psychology. *Journal of Phenomenological Psychology* 30 (2):27-44.

Adams, W. W. (1999). The interpermeation of self and world: Empirical research, existential phenomenology and transpersonal psychology. *Journal of Phenomenological Psychology* 30 (2):39-67.

Adams, W., Kendell, R. E., Hare, E. H., & Munk-Jorgensen, P. (1993). Epidemiological evidence that maternal influenza contributes to the aaetiology of schizophrenia. An analysis of Scottish, English, and Danish data. *British Journal of Psychiatry* 163:522–534.

Adkins, A. J. (1985). Cosmogony and Order in Ancient Greece. In R, Lovin (Ed.), *Cosmogony and Ethical Order* (pp. 39-66). Chicago: Chicago University.

Adler, P. A. & Adler, P. (1994) Observational techniques. *Handbook of qualitative research.* Thousand Oaks, CA: Sage.

Adolphs, R., Tranel, D., & Damasio, A. R. (1998). The human amygdala in social judgement. *Nature* 393:470–474.

REFERENCES

Afifi, A. A. & Azen, S. P. (1972). *Statistical analysis: a computer oriented approach*. New York: Academic Press.

Agnew, N. & Pyke, S. (1991). *The science game: an introduction to research in the social sciences*. Englewood Cliffs, NJ: Prentice-Hall.

Aguglia, E., Casacchia, M., Cassano, G. B., Faravelli, C., Ferrari, G., Giordano, P., Pancheri, P., Ravizza, L., Trabucchi, M., Bolino, F., Scarpato, A., Berardi, D., Provenzano, G., Brugnoli, R., & Rozzini, R. (1993). Double-blind study of the efficacy and safety of sertraline versus fluoxetine in major depression. *International Clinical Psychopharmacology* 8:197–202.

AHP. (2002). *Directory of Humanistic Professionals*. Retrieved February 6, 2003, from Association for Humanistic Psychology Web Site: http://www.ahpweb.org/pub/directory/menu1.html

Akbarian, S., Bunney, W. E. J., Potkin, S. G., Wigal, S. B., Hagman, J. O., Sandman, C. A., & Jones, E. G. (1993). Altered distribution of nicotinamide-adenine dinucleotide phosphate-diaphorase cells in frontal lobe of schizophrenics implies disturbances of cortical development. *Archives of General Psychiatry* 50:169–177.

Akiskal, H. S. (1985). Interaction of biologic and psychologic factors in the origin of depressive disorders. *Acta Psychiatrica Scandinavica* 319 (Suppl.): 131–139.

Alexander, M. J. (1996). Women with co-occurring addictive and mental disorders: An emerging profile of vulnerability. *American Journal of Orthopsychiatry* 66:61–70.

Alexander, P. C., Neimeyer, R. A., & Follette, V. M. (1991). Group therapy for women sexually abused as children: Controlled study and investigation of individual differences. *Journal of Interpersonal Violence* 6:218–231.

Alexander, P. C., Neimeyer, R. A., Follette, V. M., Moore, M. K., & Harter, S. (1989). A comparison of group treatments of women sexually abused as children. *Journal of Consulting and Clinical Psychology* 57:479–483.

Alford, R. R. (1998). *The craft of inquiry: Theories, method and evidence*. New York: Oxford Press.

Allport, G. W., and Ross, M. (1967). Personal religious orientation and prejudice. *Journal of Personality and Social Psychology* 5:432-42.

Altman, M. (2000). A behavioural model of path dependency: The economics of profitable inefficiency and market failure. *Journal of Socio-Economics* 29: 127-145.

REFERENCES

Anderson, P. (1974). *Passages from antiquity to feudalism.* London: New Left Books.

Andreasen, N. C. (1995). Symptoms, signs, and diagnosis of schizophrenia. *Lancet* 346:477B-481.

Andreasen, N. C. (1997a). The evolving concept of schizophrenia: From Kraepelin to the present and future. *Schizophrenia Research* 28:105–109.

Andreasen, N. C. (1997b). Linking mind and brain in the study of mental illnesses: A project for a scientific psychopathology. *Science* 275:1586–1593.

Andreasen, N. C., O'Leary, D. S., Cizadlo, T., Arndt, S., Rezai, K., Ponto, L. L., Watkins, G. L., & Hichwa, R. D. (1996). Schizophrenia and cognitive dysmetria: A positron-emission tomography study of dysfunctional prefrontal-thalamic-cerebellar circuitry. *Proceedings of the National Academy of Sciences of the United States of America* 93:9985–9990.

Angst, J., Angst, F., & Stassen, H. H. (1999). Suicide risk in patients with major depressive disorder. *Journal of Clinical Psychiatry* 60 (Suppl. 2): 57–62.

Annlson, J. (2000). Towards a clearer understanding of the meaning of "home." *Journal of Intellectual and Developmental Disabilities* 25 (4): 251-263.

Appingnanesi, R. (1995). *Postmodernism for beginners.* Cambridge: Icon.

Aristotle, & Editor: Bambrough (1969). *Politics.* New York: Penguin.

Ashman, K.M. & Baringer, P.S. (2001). *After the science wars.* London: Routledge.

Ascher, J. A., Cole, J. O., Colin, J. N., Feighner, J. P., Ferris, R. M., Fibiger, H. C., Golden, R. N., Martin, P., Potter, W. Z., Richelson, E., & Sulser, F. (1995). Bupropion: A review of its mechanism of antidepressant activity. *Journal of Clinical Psychiatry* 56:395–401.

Attkisson, C., Cook, J., Karno, M., Lehman, A., McGlashan, T. H., Meltzer, H. Y., O'Connor, M., Richardson, D., Rosenblatt, A., Wells, K., & Williams, J., & Hohmann, A. A. (1992). Clinical services research. *Schizophrenia Bulletin* 18:561–626.

Awad, G. A., Voruganti, L. N., & Heslegrave, R. J. (1997). Measuring quality of life in patients with schizophrenia. *Pharmacoeconomics* 11:32–47.

Baldessarini, R. J., Cohen, B. M., & Teicher, M. H. (1990). Pharmacological treatment. In S. T. Levy & P. T Ninan (Eds.), *Schizophrenia: Treatment of acute psychotic episodes* (pp. 61–118). Washington, DC: American Psychiatric Press.

Baldwin, D. S., & Birtwistle, J. (1998). The side effect burden associated with drug treatment of panic disorder. *Journal of Clinical Psychiatry* 59 (Suppl. 8): 39–44.

Ball, F. L., & Havassy, B. E. (1984). A survey of the problems and needs of homeless consumers of acute psychiatric services. *Hospital and Community Psychiatry* 35:917–921.

Ballenger, J. C., Davidson, J. R., Lecrubier, Y., Nutt, D. J., Bobes, J., Beidel, D. C., Ono, Y., & Westenberg, H. G. (1998). Consensus statement on social anxiety disorder from the International Consensus Group on Depression and Anxiety. *Journal of Clinical Psychiatry* 59 (Suppl. 17): 54–60.

Ballus, C. (1997). Effects of antipsychotics on the clinical and psychosocial behavior of patients with schizophrenia. *Schizophrenia Research* 28:247–255.

Bandura, A. (1977). Self-efficacy: Toward a unifying theory of behavioral change. *Psychological Review* 84:191–215.

Barash, D. P. (2000). Evolutionary Existentialism, Sociobiology, and the Meaning of Life. *BioScience* 50 (11): 1012-1017.

Barrow, J. D. (1999). *Impossibility. The limits of science and the science of limits*. London: Vintage.

Barry, W.A. & Connolly, W.J. (1982). *The Practice of Spiritual Direction*. New York: Seabury Press.

Barton, E. R. (2000). Parallels between mythopoetic men's work/men's peer group support and selected feminist's theories. In Barton, E.R. (Ed.), *Mythopoetic perspectives of men's healing work: An anthology for therapists and others*. (1 ed., pp. 3-20). Detroit: University of Michigan.

Beardslee, W. R., & Vaillant, G. (1997). Adult development. In A. Tasman, J. Kay, & J. A. Lieberman (Eds.), *Psychiatry* (Vol. 1, pp. 145–155). Philadelphia: W. B. Saunders.

Beasley, C. M., Jr., Dornseif, B. E., Bosomworth, J. C., Sayler, M. E., Rampey, A. H., Jr., Heiligenstein, J. H., Thompson, V. L., Murphy, D. J., & Masica, D. N. (1991). Fluoxetine and suicide: A meta-analysis of controlled trials of treatment for depression. *British Medical Journal* 303:685–692.

REFERENCES

Beasley, C. M., Jr., Sayler, M. E., Cunningham, G. E., Weiss, A. M., & Masica, D. N. (1990). Fluoxetine in tricyclic refractory major depressive disorder. *Journal of Affective Disorders* 20:193–200.

Bebbington, P., & Kuipers, L. (1994). The predictive utility of expressed emotion in schizophrenia: An aggregate analysis. *Psychological Medicine* 24:707–718.

Beck, A. T. (1976). *Cognitive therapy and the emotional disorders.* New York: International Universities Press.

Beck, A. T., Rush A. J., & Shaw B. F. (1979). *Cognitive therapy of depression.* New York: Guilford Press.

Bell, C. C. & Mehta, H. (1981). The misdiagnosis of black patients with manic depressive illness. *Journal of the National Medical Association 73,* 101–107.

Bell, M. D., & Lysaker, P. H. (1997). Clinical benefits of paid work activity in schizophrenia: 1-year followup. *Schizophrenia Bulletin* 23:317–328.

Bell, M. D., Lysaker, P. H., & Milstein, R. M. (1996). Clinical benefits of paid work activity in schizophrenia. *Schizophrenia Bulletin* 22:51–67.

Bell, M. D., & Ryan, E. R. (1984). Integrating psychosocial rehabilitation into the hospital psychiatric service. *Hospital and Community Psychiatry* 351017–1022.

Bellack, A. S., & Gearon, J. S. (1998). Substance abuse treatment for people with schizophrenia. *Addictive Behaviors* 23:749–766.

Bellack, A. S., Morrison, R. L., & Mueser, K. T. (1989). Social problem solving in schizophrenia. *Schizophrenia Bulletin* 15:101–116.

Bellack, A. S., & Mueser, K. T. (1993). Psychosocial treatment for schizophrenia. *Schizophrenia Bulletin* 19:317–336.

Bernstein, A. (2001). Freud and Oedipus: A new look at the Oedipus complex in the light of Freud's life. *Modern Psychoanalysis* 26 (2): 269-283.

Bhaskar, R. (1978). *A realist theory of science* (2nd ed.). New Jersey: Humanities Press.

Bierut, L. J., Heath, A. C., Bucholz, K. K., Dinwiddie, S. H., Madden, P. A., Statham, D. J., Dunne, M. P., & Martin, N. G. (1999). Major depressive disorder in a community-based twin sample: Are there different genetic and environmental contributions for men and women? *Archives of General Psychiatry* 56:557–563.

Black, D. W., Winokur, G., & Nasrallah, A. (1987). The treatment of depression: Electroconvulsive therapy v antidepressants: A naturalistic evaluation of 1,495 patients. *Comprehensive Psychiatry* 28:169–182.

Blackburn, I. M., Eunson, K. M., & Bishop, S. (1986). A two-year naturalistic follow-up of depressed patients treated with cognitive therapy, pharmacotherapy and a combination of both. *Journal of Affective Disorders* 10:67–75.

Blanchard, J. J., Mueser, K. T., & Bellack, A. S. (1998). Anhedonia, positive and negative affect, and social functioning in schizophrenia. *Schizophrenia Bulletin* 24:413–424.

Blehar, M. C., DePaulo, J. R. Jr, Gershon, E. S., Reich, T., Simpson, S. G., & Nurnberger, J. I. Jr. (1998). Women with bipolar disorder: Findings from the NIMH Genetics Initiative sample. *Psychopharmacology Bulletin* 34:239–243.

Bloom, F. E. (1993). Advancing a neurodevelopmental origin for schizophrenia. *Archives of General Psychiatry* 50:224–227.

Blumenthal, S. J. (1988). Suicide: A guide to risk factors, assessment, and treatment of suicidal patients. *Medical Clinics of North America* 72:937–971.

Blumenthal, S. J. (1994a). Gender differences in mental disorders. *Journal of Clinical Psychiatry* 3:453–458.

Blumenthal, S. J. (1994b). Women and depression. *Journal of Women's Health* 3:467–453.

Bonvecchi, O. C. (1999). Sophia-analysis and the existential unconscious. *International Journal of Psychotherapy* 4 (1): 79-85.

Botton, A. (2000). *The consolations of philosophy*. Hamish: Hamilton.

Bowden, C. L., Brugger, A. M., Swann, A. C., Calabrese, J. R., Janicak, P. G., Petty, F., Dilsaver, S. C., Davis, J. M., Rush, A. J., Small, J. G., Garza-Treviño, E. S., Risch, S. C., Goodnick, P. J., & Morris, D. D. (1994). Efficacy of divalproex vs lithium and placebo in the treatment of mania. The Depakote Mania Study Group. *Journal of the American Medical Association* 271:918–924.

Bracha, H. S. (1991). Aetiology of structural asymmetry in schizophrenia: An alternative hypothesis. *Schizophrenia Bulletin* 17:551–553.

REFERENCES

Braun, C. M., Lapierre, D., Hodgins, S., Toupin, J., Leveille, S., & Constantineau, C. (1995). Neurological soft signs in schizophrenia: Are they related to negative or positive symptoms, neuropsychological performance and violence? *Archives of Clinical Neuropsychology* 10:489–509.

Brawman-Mintzer, O., & Lydiard, R. B. (1996). Generalized anxiety disorder: Issues in epidemiology. *Journal of Clinical Psychiatry* 57 (Suppl. 7):3–8.

Brazo, P., & Dollfus, S. (1997). Syndromic and diagnostic heterogeneity of schizophrenia. *Encephale* 23:20–24.

Breggin, P. R., & Breggin, G. R. (1994). *Talking back to Prozac*. New York: St. Martin's Press.

Breiter, H. C., Etcoff, N. L., Whalen, P. J., Kennedy, W. A., Rauch, S. L., Buckner, R. L., Strauss, M. M., Hyman, S. E., & Rosen, B. R. (1996). Response and habituation of the human amygdala during visual processing of facial expression. *Neuron* 17:875–887.

Brekke, J. S., & Barrio, C. (1997). Cross-ethnic symptom differences in schizophrenia: The influence of culture and minority status. *Schizophrenia Bulletin* 23:305–316.

Brekke, J. S., Raine, A., & Thomson, C. (1995). Cognitive and psychophysiological correlates of positive, negative, and disorganized symptoms in the schizophrenia spectrum. *Psychiatry Research* 57:241–250.

Breslau, N., Davis, G. C., Andreski, P., & Peterson, E. (1991). Traumatic events and posttraumatic stress disorder in an urban population of young adults. *Archives of General Psychiatry* 48:216–222.

Breslau, N., Kessler, R. C., Chilcoat, H. D., Schultz, L. R., Davis, G. C., & Andreski, P. (1998). Trauma and posttraumatic stress disorder in the community: The 1996 Detroit Area Survey of Trauma. *Archives of General Psychiatry* 55:626–632.

Buchanan, R. W., Breier, A., Kirkpatrick, B., Elkashef, A., Munson, R. C., Gellad, F., Carpenter, W. T., Jr. (1993). Structural abnormalities in deficit and non-deficit schizophrenia. *American Journal of Psychiatry, 150*, 59–65.

Buckley, P. F. (1997). New dimensions in the pharmacologic treatment of schizophrenia and related psychoses. *Journal of Clinical Pharmacology* 37:363–378.

Burke, K. C., Burke, J. D., Jr., Regier, D. A., & Rae, D. S. (1990). Age at the onset of selected mental disorders in five community populations. *Archives of General Psychiatry* 47:511–518.

Burke, M. J., Silkey, B., & Preskorn, S. H. (1994). Pharmacoeconomic considerations when evaluating treatment options for major depressive disorder. *Journal of Clinical Psychiatry* 55 (Suppl. A): 42–52.

Bymaster, F. P., Rasmussen, K., Calligaro, D. O., Nelson, D. L., DeLapp, N. W., Wong, D. T., & Moore, N. A. (1997). In vitro and in vivo biochemistry of olanzapine: A novel, atypical antipsychotic drug. *Journal of Clinical Psychiatry* 58 (Suppl. 10): 28–36.

Cadenhead, K. S., Geyer, M. A., Butler, R. W., Perry, W., Sprock, J., & Braff, D. L. (1997). Information processing deficits of schizophrenia patients: Relationship to clinical ratings, gender and medication status. *Schizophrenia Research* 28:51–62.

Calabrese, J. R., & Delucchi, G. A. (1990). Spectrum of efficacy of valproate in 55 patients with rapid-cycling bipolar disorder. *American Journal of Psychiatry* 147:431–434.

Calev, A. (1994). Neuropsychology and ECT: Past and future research trends. *Psychopharmacology Bulletin* 30:461–469.

Callahan, D. (1999). Balancing efficiency and need in allocating resources to the care of persons with serious mental illness. *Psychiatric Services* 50:664–666.

Callahan, E. J., Bertakis, K. D., Azari, R., Robbins, J., Helms, L. J., & Miller, J. (1996). The influence of depression on physician-patient interaction in primary care. *Family Medicine* 28:346–351.

Campbell, A. (1981). *The sense of well-being in America: Recent patterns and trends.* New York: McGraw-Hill.

Campbell, A., Converse, P., & Rodgers, W. (1976). *The Quality of American Life.* New York: Russell Sage Foundation.

Campion, N., & Rossi, JP (2001). Associative and Causal Constraints in the Process of Generating Predictive Inference. *Discourse Processes* 31 (2):263-291.

Caveny, C. M. (2003). Wholesomeness, Holiness and Hairspray. *America* 188 (7): 15-19.

Cazzullo, C. L., Bertrando, P., Clerici, C., Bressi, C., Da Ponte, C., & Albertini, E. (1989). The efficacy of an information group intervention on relatives of schizophrenics. *International Journal of Social Psychiatry* 35:313–323.

Cenkner, W. (1997). *Evil and the response of world religions* (1 ed.). New York: Paragon.

REFERENCES

Cetina, K. K. (1999). Epistemic cultures. How the sciences make knowledge. London: Harvard Press

Center for Mental Health Services. (1995). Double jeopardy: Persons with mental illnesses in the criminal justice system. Rockville, MD: Author.

Center for Mental Health Services. (1996). Consumer Affairs Bulletin, 1 (1).

Center for Mental Health Services. (1997). Cultural competence standards in managed mental health care for four underserved/underrepresented racial/ethnic groups (Final report from Working Groups on Cultural Competence in Managed Mental Health Care). Rockville, MD: Author.

Center for Mental Health Services. (1998). *Electroconvulsive therapy background paper* (DHHS Publication No. SMA 98-3201). Vienna, VA: Research-Abele, Inc.

Chakos, M. H., Alvir, J. M., Woerner, M. G., Koreen, A., Geisler, S., Mayerhoff, D., Sobel, S., Kane, J. M., Borenstein, M., & Lieberman, J. A. (1996). Incidence and correlates of tardive dyskinesia in first episode of schizophrenia. *Archives of General Psychiatry* 53:313–319.

Chamberlin, J., & Rogers, J. A. (1990). Planning a community-based mental health system. Perspective of service recipients. *American Psychologist* 45:1241–1244.

Chambless, D. K., Baker, M. J., Baucom, D. H., Beutler, L. E., et al. (1998). Update on empirically validated therapies II. *The Clinical Psychologist* 51:3–16.

Charney, D. S., & Deutch, A. (1996). A functional neuroanatomy of anxiety and fear: Implications for the pathophysiology and treatment of anxiety disorders. *Critical Reviews in Neurobiology* 10:419–446.

Chouinard, G. (1988). The use of benzodiazepines in the treatment of manic-depressive illness. *Journal of Clinical Psychiatry* 49 (Suppl.): 15–20.

Christensen, A., & Heavey, C. L. (1999). Interventions for couples. *Annual Review of Psychology* 50:165B-190.

Chung, M. C. (1999). Revisiting and contrasting thought between Descartes and Spinoza in the light of psychotherapy. *Counseling Psychology Quarterly, 12*(1), 49-56. Ciompi, L. (1980). Catamnestic long-term study on the course of life and aging of schizophrenics. *Schizophrenia Bulletin* 6:606–618.

Claghorn, J. L., & Feighner, J. P. (1993). A double-blind comparison of paroxetine with imipramine in the long-term treatment of depression. *Journal of Clinical Psychopharmacology* 13:23S–27S.

Clark, L. A., Watson, D., & Mineka, S. (1994). Temperament, personality, and the mood and anxiety disorders. *Journal of Abnormal Psychology* 103:103–116.

Clayton, P. J., & Darvish, H. S. (1979). Course of depressive symptoms following the stress of bereavement. In J. E. Barrett, R. M. Rose, & G. Klerman (Eds.), *Stress and mental disorder* (pp. 121–136). New York: Raven.

Clerc, G. E., Ruimy, P., & Verdeau-Palles, J. (1994). A double-blind comparison of venlaflaxine and fluoxetine in patients hospitalized for major depression and melancholia. The Venlafaxine French Inpatient Study Group. *International Clinical Psychopharmacology* 9:139–143.

Cohen, J. (1988). *Statistical Power Analysis for the Behavioral Sciences* (2nd ed.). New Jersey: Lawrence Earlbaum Associates.

Collins, P. H. (1992). *Black feminist thought.* Chichester: John Wiley.

Cooper, L. (2001). Beyond the Tripartite Soul: The Dynamic Psychology of the Republic. *Review of Politics* 63 (2): 341-360.

Cottingham, J. (2002). Descartes and the Voluntariness of Belief. *Monist* 85 (3): 343-360.

Cropsey, J. (1995). *Plato's World: Man's Place in the Cosmos.* Chicago: Chicago University.

Crismon, M. L., Trivedi, M., Pigott, T. A., Rush, A. J., Hirschfeld, R. M., Kahn, D. A., DeBattista, C., Nelson, J. C., Nierenberg, A. A., Sackeim, H. A., & Thase, M. A. (1999). The Texas Medication Algorithm Project: Report of the Texas Consensus Conference Panel on Medication Treatment of Major Depressive Disorder. *Journal of Clinical Psychiatry* 60:142–156.

Crow, T. J. (1985). The two-syndrome concept: Origins and current status. *Schizophrenia Bulletin* 11:471–486.

Crow, T. J. (1995). Brain changes and negative symptoms in schizophrenia. *Psychopathology* 28:18–21.

Csernansky, J. G., & Grace, A. A. (1998). New models of the pathophysiology of schizophrenia: Editors' introduction. *Schizophrenia Bulletin* 24:185–187.

REFERENCES

Curley, E. (1985). *The Collected Works of Spinoza* (1 ed.). New York: Princeton Press.

D'Zurilla, T. J., Nezu, A. M., & Maydeu-Olivares, A. (2002). *SPSI-R Social Problem-Solving Inventory-Revised - Technical Manual.* Toronto: Multi-Health Systems.

Damasio, A. (1999). *The feeling of what happens. Body, emotion and the making of consciousness.* London: William Heinemann.

Dancy, J. & Sosa, E. (1993). *A companion to epistemology.* Oxford: Blackwell.

Dassori, A. M., Miller, A. L., & Saldana, D. (1995). Schizophrenia among Hispanics: Epidemiology, phenomenology, course, and outcome. *Schizophrenia Bulletin* 21:303–312.

Davidson, J. (1989). Seizures and bupropion: A review. *Journal of Clinical Psychiatry* 50:256-261.

Davidson, J. R. (1998). Pharmacotherapy of social anxiety disorder. *Journal of Clinical Psychiatry* 59 (Suppl. 17): 47–53.

Davis, J. M., Barter, J. T., & Kane, J. M. (1989). The natural course of schizophrenia and effective maintenance drug treatment. In H. I. Kaplan & B. J. Sadock (Eds.), *Comprehensive textbook of psychiatry* (Vol. 5, pp. 1591–1626). Baltimore: Williams & Wilkins.

Davis, M. (1997). Neurobiology of fear responses: The role of the amygdala. *Journal of Neuropsychiatry and Clinical Neurosciences* 9:382–402.

Dawlans, K. (1995). Gender differences in psychiatry: Epidemiology and drug response. *CNS Drugs* 3:393–407.

De Andrade, C. E. (2000). Becoming the wise woman: A study of women's journey through midlife transformation. *University microfilms international – Dissertation* 61:1109.

Descartes, Rene' (). *Meditatio on First Philosophy.* New York: .

Dillon, M. (2000). Dialogues with Death: The Last Days of Socrates and the Buddha. *Philosophy East and West* 50 (4): 525-560.

Dincin, J. (1975). Psychiatric rehabilitation. *Schizophrenia Bulletin* 13:131–147.

Dincin, J., & Witheridge, T. F. (1982). Psychiatric rehabilitation as a deterrent to recividism. *Hospital and Community Psychiatry* 33:645–650.

Dixon, L. B., Hackman, A., & Lehman, A. F. (1997). Consumers as staff in assertive community treatment programs. *Administration and Policy in Mental Health* 25:199–208.

Dixon, L. B., Lehman, A. F., & Levine, J. (1995). Conventional antipsychotic medications for schizophrenia. *Schizophrenia Bulletin* 21:567–577.

Dixon, L., Postrado, L., Delahanty, J., Fischer, P. J., & Lehman, A. (1999). The association of medical comorbidity in schizophrenia with poor physical and mental health. *Journal of Nervous and Mental Disease* 187:496–502.

Dixon, L. B., Stewart, B., Krauss, N., Robbins, J., Hackman, A., & Lehman, A. F. (1998). The participation of families of homeless persons with severe mental illness in an outreach intervention. *Community Mental Health Journal* 34:251–259.

Dixon, L., Weiden, P., Delahanty, J., Goldberg, R., Postrado, L., Lucksted, A., & Lehman, A. (in press-a). Diabetes and schizophrenia. *Schizophrenia Bulletin*.

Dixon, L., Wohlheiter, K., & Thompson, D. (in press-b). Medical management of schizophrenia. In J. Lieberman & R. Murray (Eds.), *Comprehensive care of schizophrenia*. London: Martin Dunitz Publishers.

Dobson, K. S. (1989). A meta-analysis of the efficacy of cognitive therapy for depression. *Journal of Consulting and Clinical Psychology* 57:414–419.

Docherty, N. M., DeRosa, M., & Andreasen, N. C. (1996). Communication disturbances in schizophrenia and mania. *Archives of General Psychiatry* 53:358–364.

Donlon, P. T., Hopkin, J. T., Tupin, J. P., Wicks, J. J., Wahba, M., & Meadow, A. (1980). Haloperidol for acute schizophrenic patients. An evaluation of three oral regimens. *Archives of General Psychiatry* 37:691–695.

Donlon, P. T., Meadow, A., Tupin, J. P., & Wahba, M. (1978). High vs standard dosage fluphenazine HCL in acute schizophrenia. *Journal of Clinical Psychiatry* 39:800–804.

Doogan, D. P., & Caillard, V. (1992). Sertraline in the prevention of depression. *British Journal of Psychiatry* 160:217–222.

Dorsa, D. (1995). *The importance of ritual to children*. Dissertation International: Us Microfiles.

Drevets, W. C. (1998). Functional neuroimaging studies of depression: The anatomy of melancholia. *Annual Review of Medicine* 49:341–361.

Drury, V., Birchwood, M., Cochrane, R., & Macmillan, F. (1996). Cognitive therapy and recovery from acute psychosis: A controlled trial: II. Impact on recovery time. *British Journal of Psychiatry* 169:602–607.

Druss, B. G., & Rosenheck, R. A. (1998). Mental disorders and access to medical care in the United States. American Journal of Psychiatry 155:1775–1777.

DSM-IV. See American Psychiatric Association (1994).

Edwards, A. (1991). Clipping the wings off the Enneagram: A study of people's perceptions of a ninefold personality typology. *Social Behavior and Personality* 19:11-20.

Elkin, I., Shea, M. T., Watkins, J. T., Imber, S. D., Sotsky, S. M., Collins, J. F., Glass, D. R., Pilkonis, P. A., Leber, W. R., Docherty, J. P., Fiester, S. J., & Parloff, M. B. (1989). National Institute of Mental Health Treatment of Depression Collaborative Research Program. General effectiveness of treatments. *Archives of General Psychiatry* 46:971–982.

Ellison, C. W. (1993). Spiritual Well-being: Conceptualization and Measurement. *Journal of Psychology and Theology* 11 (4): 330-340.

Ellenbroek, B. A., & Cools, A. R. (1998). Mini-review. The neurodevelopmental hypothesis of schizophrenia: Clinical evidence and animal models. *Neuroscience Research Communications* 22:127–136.

Endler, N. S., & Flett, G. L. (2002). In (Ed.), *EMAS Social Anxiety Scales* (p.). Los Angeles: Western Psychological Services.

Evans, S. C. (1990). *Soren Kiekegaard's Christian Psychology*. Vancouver: Regent College .

Eysenck, H. K., & Eysenck, S. B. (1975). *Eysenck personality questionnaire manual*. San Diego: Educational and Industrial Testing Service.

Fancher, R. E. (1979). *Pioneers of Psychology*. New York: Norton.

Featherman, D. & Rockwell, R. (1992). Social science research council. *Encyclopedia of Sociology, vol.4*. New York: MacMillan.

Federal Interagency Task Force on Homelessness and Mental Illness. (1992). *Outcasts on Main Street*. Washington, DC: Federal Interagency Task Force on Homelessness and Mental Illness.

Feighner, J. P. (1999). Mechanism of action of antidepressant medications. *Journal of Clinical Psychiatry* 60 (Suppl. 4): 4–11.

REFERENCES

Felker, B., Yazel, J. J., & Short, D. (1996). Mortality and medical comorbidity among psychiatry patients: A review. *Psychiatric Services* 47:1356–1363.

Felton, C. J., Stastny, P., Shern, D. L., Blanch, A., Donahue, S. A., Knight, E., & Brown, C. (1995). Consumers as peer specialists on intensive case management teams: Impact on client outcomes. *Psychiatric Services* 46:1037–1044.

Fine, G. (1992). The culture of production: Aesthetic choices and constraints in culinary work. *American Journal of Sociology* 97:1268-1294.

Firestone, R. W., & Firestone, L. A. (1996). *Firestone Assessment of Self-Destructive Thoughts*. New York: Harcourt Brace.

Flavell, J. H. (1963). *The developmental psychology of Jean Piaget*. New York: Van Nostrand.

Foucault, M. (1997). *The order of things*. London: Routledge.

Fowler, J. (1981). *Stages of Faith: The Psychology of Human Development and the Quest for Meaning*. San Francisco: HarperCollins.

French, S. & Joseph, S. (1999). Religiosity and its association with happiness, purpose in life, and self-actualization. *Mental Health, Religion and Culture* 2:117-120.

Fry, P.S. (2000) Religious involvement, spirituality and personal meaning for life: Existential predictors of psychological well-being in community residing and institutional care elders. *Aging and Mental Health* 4:375-387.

Fukuzako, H., Fukuzako, T., Takeuchi, K., Ohbo, Y., Ueyama, K., Takigawa, M., & Fujimoto, T. (1996). Phosphorus magnetic resonance spectroscopy in schizophrenia: Correlation between membrane phospholipid metabolism in the temporal lobe and positive symptoms. *Progress in Neuropsychopharmacology and Biological Psychiatry* 20:629–640.

Gaebel, W., Frick, U., Kopcke, W., Linden, M., Muller, P., Muller-Spahn, F., Pietzcker, A., & Tegeler, J. (1993). Early neuroleptic intervention in schizophrenia: Are prodromal symptoms valid predictors of relapse? *British Journal of Psychiatry. Supplement* 21:8–12.

Galanter, M. (1988). Zealous self-help groups as adjuncts to psychiatric treatment: A study of Recovery, Inc. *American Journal of Psychiatry* 145:1248–1253.

Gallhofer, B., Bauer, U., Lis, S., Krieger, S., & Gruppe, H. (1996). Cognitive dysfunction in schizophrenia: Comparison of treatment with atypical antipsychotic agents and conventional neuroleptic drugs. *European Neuropsychopharmacology* 6 (Suppl. 2): S13–S20.

Gardner, E. A., & Johnston, J. A. (1985). Bupropion—An antidepressant without sexual pathophysiological action. *Journal of Clinical Psychopharmacology* 5:24–29.

Gaultieri, A. (1968). The Resurrection: An Existential Verification. *Christian Century* 85:451-453.

Genova, J. (1995). *Wittgenstein: a way of seeing*. London: Routledge.

Gill, D. (1991). Socrates and Jesus in non-retaliation and love of enemies. *Horizons, 18,* 246-262. Goldman, H., Lehman, A., Morrissey, J., Newman, S., Frank, R., & Steinwachs, D. (1990a). Design for the national evaluation of the Robert Wood Johnson Foundation program on chronic mental illness. *Hospital and Community Psychiatry* 41:1217–1221.

Goldman, H., Morrissey, J., & Ridgely, M. S. (1990b). Form and function of mental health authorities at RWJ Foundation program sites: Preliminary observations. *Hospital and Community Psychiatry* 41:1222–1230.

Goldman, H. H., Morrissey, J. P., & Ridgely, M. S. (1994a). Evaluating the Robert Wood Johnson Foundation program on chronic mental illness. *Milbank Quarterly* 72:37–47.

Goldman, H., Morrissey, J., & Ridgely, M. S. (1994b). Evaluating the program on chronic mental illness (RWJ PCMI). *Milbank Quarterly* 72:37–48.

Goldman-Rakic, P. S., & Selemon, L. D. (1997). Functional and anatomical aspects of prefrontal pathology in schizophrenia. *Schizophrenia Bulletin* 23:437–458.

Goldstein, M. J. (1995a). Psychoeducation and relapse prevention. *International Clinical Psychopharmacology* 9 (Suppl. 5):59–69.

Goldstein, M. J. (1995b). Transactional processes associated with relatives' expressed emotion. *International Journal of Mental Health* 24:76–96.

Gould, S. J. (1999). *Rocks of ages: science and religion in the fullness of life*. New York: Ballantine.

Greenfield, S. (2000). *The private life of the brain*. London: Allen Lane/Penguin.

Grinnell, F. (1987). *The Scientific Attitude*. Boulder, CO: Westview.

Gross, D. (1984). Time allocation: A tool for the study of cultural behaviour. *Annual Review of Anthropology* 13:519-558.

Guba, E & Lincoln. Y. (1994) Competing paradigms in qualitative research. IN *Handbook of qualitative research*. Thousand Oaks, CA: Sage.

Gusfield, J (1976). The literary rhetoric of science. *American Sociological Review, 41:* 16-34. Gunderson, J. G., Frank, A. F., Katz, H. M., Vannicelli, M. L., Frosch, J. P., & Knapp, P. H. (1984). Effects of psychotherapy in schizophrenia: II. Comparative outcome of two forms of treatment. *Schizophrenia Bulletin* 10:564-598.

Gupta, S., Andreasen, N. C., Arndt, S., Flaum, M., Hubbard, W. C., & Ziebell, S. (1997). The Iowa longitudinal study of recent onset psychosis: One-year follow-up of first episode patients. *Schizophrenia Research* 23:1-13.

Hackney, C.H. & Sanders, G.S. (2003). Religiosity and Mental Health: A Meta-Analysis of Recent Studies. *Journal for the Scientific Study of Religion* 42 (1): 43-55.

Hafner, H., an der Heiden, W., Behrens, S., Gattaz, W. F., Hambrecht, M., Loffler, W., Maurer, K., Munk-Jorgensen, P., Nowotny, B., Riecher-Rossler, A., & Stein, A. (1998). Causes and consequences of the gender difference in age at onset of schizophrenia. *Schizophrenia Bulletin* 24:99-113.

Hamel, S., LeClerc, G., & LeFrancois, R. (2003). A psychological outlook on the concept of transcendent actualization. *International Journal for the Psychology of Religion* 13 (1): 3-15.

Harre, R. (1998). *The singularity of self.* London: Sage.

Heath, G. (2000). A constructivist attempt to talk to the field, *International Journal of Psychotherapy* 5 (1): 11-35.

Hermanson, M. (2000). Hybrid Identity Formations in Muslim America. *Muslim World* 90:148-190.

Hill, W. (1975). Does God know the future: Aquinas and some moderns. *Theological Studies, 35,* 3-18. Himmelhoch, J. M., Thase, M. E., Mallinger, A. G., & Houck, P. (1991). Tranylcypromine versus imipramine in anergic bipolar depression. *American Journal of Psychiatry* 148:910-916.

Hirschfeld, R. M., Keller, M. B., Panico, S., Arons, B. S., Barlow, D., Davidoff, F., Endicott, J., Froom, J., Goldstein, M., Gorman, J. M., Marek, R. G., Maurer, T. A., Meyer, R., Phillips, K., Ross, J., Schwenk, T. L., Sharfstein, S. S., Thase, M. E., & Wyatt, R. J. (1997). The National Depressive and Manic-Depressive Association consensus statement on the undertreatment of depression. *Journal of the American Medical Association* 277:333–340.

Hirschfeld, R., & Shea, T. (1992). Personality. In E. Paykel (Ed.), *Handbook of affective disorders* (pp. 185–194). New York: Guilford Press.

Hobson, P (2002). *The cradle of thought. Exploring the origins of thinking.* London, Macmillan.

Ho, B. C., Nopoulos, P., Flaum, M., Arndt, S., & Andreasen, N. C. (1998). Two-year outcome in first-episode schizophrenia: Predictive value of symptoms for quality of life. *American Journal of Psychiatry* 155:1196–1201.

Hoffman, F. L., & Mastrianni, X. (1993). The role of supported education in the inpatient treatment of young adults: A two-site comparison. *Psychosocial Rehabilitation Journal* 17:109–119.

Hogarty, G. E., Anderson, C. M., & Reiss, D. J. (1987). Family psychoeducation, social skills training, and medication in schizophrenia: The long and short of it. *Psychopharmacology Bulletin* 23:12–13.

Hogarty, G. E., Greenwald, D., Ulrich, R. F., Kornblith, S. J., DiBarry, A. L., Cooley, S., Carter, M., & Flesher, S. (1997). Three-year trials of personal therapy among schizophrenic patients living with or independent of family, II: Effects on adjustment of patients. *American Journal of Psychiatry* 154:1514–1524.

Humphrey, N. (1992). *A history of the mind.* London: Macmillan.

Husserl, E. (1962). The Thesis of the Natural Standpoint and Its Suspension. In R. Solomon (Ed.), *Phenomenology and Existentialism* (pp. 112-117). New York: Harper and Row.

Inayama, Y., Yoneda, H., Sakai, T., Ishida, T., Nonomura, Y., Kono, Y., Takahata, R., Koh, J., Sakai, J., Takai, A., Inada, Y., & Asaba, H. (1996). Positive association between a DNA sequence variant in the serotonin 2A receptor gene and schizophrenia. *American Journal of Medical Genetics* 67:103–105.

Ingram, R. E., Miranda, J., & Segal, Z. V. (1998). *Cognitive vulnerability to depression.* New York: Guilford Press.

Institute of Medicine (1994). Reducing risks for mental disorders: Frontiers for preventive intervention research. Washington, DC: National Academy Press.

Institute of Medicine (1995). Development of medications for the treatment of opiate and cocaine addictions: Issues for the government and private sector. Washington, DC: National Academy Press.

Institute of Medicine. (1996). *Understanding violence against women.* Washington, DC: National Academy Press.

Institute of Medicine (1998). *Violence in families: Assessing prevention and treatment programs.* Washington, DC: National Academy Press.

Ivey, A.E., Ivey, M.B. & Simek – Morgan, L. (1993). *Counseling and psychotherapy a multicultural perspective.* Needham Heights, MA: Allyn & Bacon.

Jacob, A. (1999). Cosmology and Ethics in the Religions of the Peoples of the Ancient Near East. *The Mankind Quarterly* XL (1): 95-119.

Jacobson, L., & Sapolsky, R. (1991). The role of the hippocampus in feedback regulation of the hypothalmic-pituitary-adrenocortical axis. *Endocrine Reviews* 12:118–134.

Jann, M. W., Chang, W. H., Lam, Y. W., Hwu, H. G., Lin, H. N., Chen, H., Chen, T. Y., Lin, S. K., Chien, C. P., Davis, C. M., Ereshefsky, L., Sakland, S. R., Richards, A. L., & Shulteis, W. M. (1992). Comparison of haloperidol and reduced haloperidol plasma levels in four different ethnic populations. *Progress in Neuro- Psychopharmacology and Biological Psychiatry* 16:193–202.

Jeffs, T. (2003). Quest for knowledge begins with a recognition of shared ignorance. *Adults Learning* 14 (6): 28.

Johnson, L. D. (1975). *Israel's Wisdom – Live and Learn.* Nashville: Broadman.

Jorgensen, P. (1998). Early signs of psychotic relapse in schizophrenia. *British Journal of Psychiatry* 172:327–330.

Kaiser, W. C. (1979). *Ecclesiastes: Total Life.* Chicago: Moody.

Kane, J. M. (1985). Antipsychotic drug side effects: Their relationship to dose. *Journal of Clinical Psychiatry* 46:16–21.

Kane, J. M. (1989). The current status of neuroleptic therapy. *Journal of Clinical Psychiatry* 50:322–328.

REFERENCES

Kareem, F. (2000). *Values for a Godless age. The story of the United Kingdom's New Bill of Rights.* London: Penguin.

Keeler, M. L., & Swanson, H. L. (2001). Does Strategy Knowledge Influence Working Memory in Children with Mathematical Disabilities? *Journal of Learning Disabilities* 34 (5): 418-435.

Keijzer, F. A. (2000). Modeling human experience?! *Philosophical Psychology* 13 (2): 239-245.

Keller, M. B., Lavori, P. W., Kane, J. M., Gelenberg, A. J., Rosenbaum, J. F., Walzer, E. A., & Baker, L. A. (1992). Subsyndromal symptoms in bipolar disorder. A comparison of standard and low serum levels of lithium. *Archives of General Psychiatry* 49:371–376.

Keller, M. B., & Shapiro, R. W. (1982). "Double depression": Superimposition of acute depressive episodes on chronic depressive disorders. *American Journal of Psychiatry* 139:438–442.

Kendler, K. S., & Diehl, S. R. (1993). The genetics of schizophrenia: A current, genetic-epidemiologic perspective. *Schizophrenia Bulletin* 19:261–285.

Kendler, K. S., Heath, A. C., Martin, N. G., & Eaves, L. J. (1987). Symptoms of anxiety and symptoms of depression. Same genes, different environments? *Archives of General Psychiatry* 44:451–457.

Kiel, J. (1999). Reshaping Maslow's hierarchy of needs to reflect today's educational and managerial philosophies. *Journal of Instructional Psychology* 26 (3):167-168.

Kilman, R. H., & Saxton, M. J. (1991). *The Kilmann-Saxton Culture Gap Survey.* Tuxedo, N.Y.: XICOM CORP.

Krieger, N., Rowley, D. L., Herman, A. A., Avery, B., & Phillips, M. T. (1993). Racism, sexism, and social class: Implications for studies of health, disease, and well-being. *American Journal of Preventive Medicine* 9 (Suppl.): 82–122.

Kukopulos, A., Reginaldi, D., Laddomada, P., Floris, G., Serra, G., & Tondo, L. (1980). Course of the manic-depressive cycle and changes caused by treatment. *Pharmakopsychiatrie Neuro-Psychopharmakologie* 13:156–167.

Kushner, H. (1986). *When all you've ever wanted isn't enough.* New York: Summit Books.

Lam, D. H. (1991). Psychosocial family intervention in schizophrenia: A review of empirical studies. *Psychological Medicine* 21:423–441.

REFERENCES

Lam, Y. W., Jann, M. W., Chang, W. H., Yu, H. S., Lin, S. K., Chen, H., & Davis, C. M. (1995). Intra- and interethnic variability in reduced haloperidol to haloperidol ratios. *Journal of Clinical Pharmacology* 35:128–136.

Lamarque, V. (1996). [Hematologic effects of clozapine: A review of the international experience]. *Encephale* 22 (6): 35–36.

Lamb, H. R., & Weinberger, L. E. (1998). Persons with severe mental illness in jails and prisons: A review. *Psychiatric Services* 49:483–492.

Languilla, N. T. (1993). On location at Socrates feet or the immanence of transcendence. *Telos* 96:143-147.

Lantz, J. (2000). Phenomenological Reflection and time in Viktor Frankl's Existential Psychotherapy. *Journal of Phenomenological Psychology* 31 (2): 220-232.

Lasky, E. (1975). *Humanness and Exploration into Mythologies about Women and Men.* New York: MSS Information Corp.

Lederman, M & Bartsch, I. (Eds) (2001). *The gender and science reader.* London: Routledge.

Levenson, M. R., & Khilwati, A. H. (1999). Mystical self-annihilation: Method and meaning. *International Journal for the Psychology of Religion* 9 (4): 251-258.

Lieberson, S. (1991). Small N's and big conclusions: An examination of the reasoning of comparative studies based on a small number of cases. *Social Forces* 70:307-320.

Lillegard, N. (2000). Passion and Reason: Aristotelian Strategies in Kierkegaard's Ethics. *Journal of Religious Ethics* 30 (2): 251-273.

Little, D. (1991). *Varieties of social explanation. An introduction to the philosophy of science.* Boulder, CO: Westview.

Lin, K. M., Anderson, D., & Poland, R. E. (1995). Ethnicity and psychopharmacology. Bridging the gap. *Psychiatric Clinics of North America* 18:635–647.

Lin, K. M., Anderson, D., & Poland, R. E. (1997). Ethnic and cultural considerations in psychopharmacotherapy. In D. Dunner (Ed.), *Current psychiatric therapy* (2nd ed., pp. 75–81). Philadelphia: W. B. Saunders.

Longino, H. (1990). *Science as social knowledge: values and objectivity in scientific inquiry.* Princeton, NJ: Princeton University Press.

REFERENCES

Lyotard, J (1984). *The postmodern condition: a report on knowledge.* Manchester: Manchester University.

MacCoby, M. (2002). Towards a Science of Social Character. *International Forum on Psychoanalysis* 11 (1): 33-45.

MacHovec, F. J. (1984). Current Therapies and the Ancient East. *American Journal of Psychotherapy* 38 (1): 87-96.

Mageo, J. M. (2002). Intertextual interpretation, fantasy and Samoan dreams. *Culture and Psychology* 8 (4): 417-448.

May, R. (1991). *Cry for Myth.* New York: W W Norton.

McDowell, M. J. (2001). Principles of Organization: A dynamic systems view of the archetype as such. *Journal of Analytical Psychology* 46 (4): 637-654.

McNamara, P. H., & St. George, A. (1979). Measures of Religiosity and the Quality of Life. In D.O. Moberg (Ed.), *Spiritual Well-being: Sociological Perspectives* (p.). Washington, D.C.: University Press of America.

McPherson, C. W. (2000). Augustine our Contemporary. *CrossCurrents* 50:170-177.

McWilliam, J. (1995). Language and Love: Introducing Augustine's Religious Thought through the Confessions Story. *Theological Studies* 56:814-815.

Merton, R (1973). *The sociology of science.* Chicago: Chicago University Press.

Meredith, L. S., Wells, K. B., & Camp, P. (1994). Clinician specialty and treatment style for depressed outpatients with and without medical comorbidities. *Archives of Family Medicine* 3:1065–1072.

Meredith, L. S., Wells, K. B., Kaplan, S. H., & Mazel, R. M. (1996). Counseling typically provided for depression. Role of clinician specialty and payment system. *Archives of General Psychiatry* 53:905–912.

Michalon, M. (2001). "Selflessness" in the service of the Ego: Contributions, Limitations and Dangers of Buddhist Psychology for Western Psychology. *Journal of Psychotherapy* 55 (2): 202-219.

Mickley, J.R., Carson, V., & Soeken, K.L. (1995) Religion and adult mental health: State of science in nursing. *Issues in Mental Health Nursing* 16:345-360.

Miller, G. A. (1995). *THE SASSI MANUAL.* New York: Addictions Research and Consultation.

REFERENCES

Miller, J. & Tewksbury, R (2000). *Extreme methods: Innovative approaches to social science research.* New York: Addison, Wesley, Longman.

Montana, C. (2002). Schizophrenia and Story: Intimate threads weaving psyche's fabric. *Dissertations International* 63:2013.

Moon, G. (2002). Spiritual Direction: Meaning, Purpose, and Implications for Mental Health Professionals. *Journal of Psychology and Theology* 30 (4): 264-275.

Mosher, L. R., & Menn, A. (1978). Community residential treatment for schizophrenia: Two year follow-up. *Hospital and Community Psychiatry* 29:715-723.

Mowbray, C. T., Leff, S., Warren, R., McCrohan, N. M., & Bybee, D. (1997). Enhancing vocational outcomes for persons with psychiatric disabilities: A new paradigm. In S. W. Henggeler & A. B. Santos (Eds.), *Innovative approaches for difficult-to-treat populations* (pp. 311-350). Washington, DC: American Psychiatric Press.

Mowbray, C. T., Moxley, D. P., Thrasher, S., Bybee, D., McCrohan, N., Harris, S., & Clover, G. (1996). Consumers as community support providers: Issues created by role innovation. *Community Mental Health Journal* 32:47-67.

Mowbray, C. T., Solomon, M., Ribisl, K. M., Ebejer, M. A., Deiz, N., Brown, W., Bandla, H., Luke, D. A., Davidson, W. S., Jr.,, & Herman, S. (1995). Treatment for

Murray, D. J. (1988). *A history of Western psychology* (2nd ed.). Englewood Cliffs, NJ: Prentice Hall.

Murray, H. A. (1971). *Thematic Apperception Test - Manual.* Cambridge, Mass.: Harvard University Press.

Nagel, T. (1986). *The view from nowhere.* Oxford: Oxford University Press.

Nagel, T. (1995). *Other minds: critical essays 1969-1994.* Oxford: Oxford University Press.

Najman, H. (2000). The writings and reception of Philo of Alexandria. In L. Johnson (Ed.), *Christianity in Jewish Terms* (pp. 99-106 & 378-397). Boulder: Westview.

Nakamura, M., Inoue, A., Hemmi, H., & Suzuki, J. (1995). Positive associations between dopamine D4 receptor polymorphism and schizophrenia. A study on two schizophrenic groups with loading and unloading. *Proceedings of the Japan Academy Series B-Physical and Biological Sciences* 71:214-243.

Narrow, W. E., Regier, D. A., Rae, D. S., Manderscheid, R. W., & Locke, B. Z. (1993). Use of services by persons with mental and addictive disorders. Findings from the National Institute of Mental Health Epidemiologic Catchment Area program. *Archives of General Psychiatry* 50:95–107

National Institute of Mental Health. (1998). *Genetics and mental disorders: Report of the National Institute of Mental Health's genetics workgroup.* Rockville, MD: Author.

National Institute on Disability and Rehabilitation Research. (1992). *Strategies to secure and maintain employment for people with long-term mental illness.* Washington, DC: Author.

National Institutes of Health, & National Institute of Mental Health. (1985). Consensus conference. Electroconvulsive therapy. *Journal of the American Medical Association* 254:2103–2108.

National Resource Center on Homelessness and Mental Illness. (1989). *Self-help programs for people who are homeless and mentally ill.* Delmar, NY: Policy Research Associates.

Nazroo, J. Y., Edwards, A. C., & Brown, G. W. (1997). Gender differences in the onset of depression following a shared life event: A study of couples. *Psychological Medicine* 27:9–19.

Neborsky, R., Janowsky, D., Munson, E., & Depry, D. (1981). Rapid treatment of acute psychotic symptoms with high- and low-dose haloperidol. Behavioral considerations. *Archives of General Psychiatry* 38:195–199.

Neeleman, J. & Lewis, G. (1994). Religious identity and comfort beliefs in three groups of psychiatric patients and a group of medical controls. *International Journal of Social Psychiatry* 40:124-134.

Neuman, L. W. (2003). *Social Research Methods* (5th ed., Rev.). New York: Allyn and Bacon.

Olfson, M., & Klerman G. L. (1992). The treatment of depression: Prescribing practices of primary care physicians and psychiatrists. *Journal of Family Practice* 35:627–635.

Olfson, M., & Klerman, G. L. (1993). Trends in the prescription of antidepressants by office-based psychiatrists. *American Journal of Psychiatry* 150:571–577.

Olsen, M & Micklin, M. (1981). *Handbook of applied sociology.* New York: Praeger.

REFERENCES

Olson, C. (1977). Existential, Social and Cosmic significance of the Upanayana rite. *Numen* 24:152-160.

Ong, A & Ward, C. (1999). The effects of sex and power schemas, attitudes toward women,, and victim resistance on rape attributions. *Journal of Applied Social Psychology* 29:362-376.

Owen, C., Rutherford, V., Jones, M., Wright, C., Tennant, C., & Smallman, A. (1996). Housing accommodation preferences of people with psychiatric disabilities. *Psychiatric Services* 47:628–632.

Owen, I. R. (1994). Introducing an Existential-Phenomenological Approach Part 2 – Theory for Practice. *Counselling Psychology Quarterly* 7 (4): 347-359.

Paloutzian, R. F., & Ellison, C. W. (1991). *Manual for the Spiritual Wellbeing Scale*. Nyack, N.Y.: Life Advance.

Parker, I (Ed.)(1999). *Deconstructing psychotherapy*. London: Sage.

Patel, S. (2002) An Analysis of Religion and Mental Health. *Canadian Journal of Psychiatry* 47 (10): 971.

Patterson, T. L., Semple, S. J., Shaw, W. S., Halpain, M., Moscona, S., Grant, I., & Jeste, D. V. (1997). Self-reported social functioning among older patients with schizophrenia. *Schizophrenia Research* 27:199–210.

Pedersen, P.T. (1997). *Culture-centered counselling interventions*. London: Sage.

Pekarsky, D. (1994). Socratic Teaching: A Critical Assessment. *Journal of Moral Education* 23 (2): 119-133.

Penticoff, J. (2002). A personal journey through the Mosaic of Thought. *Journal of Adolescent and Adult Literacy* 45 (7): 634-670.

Phillips, A (2000). *Promises, promises*. London: Faber & Faber.

Pietersma, H. (2000). *Phenomenological epistemology*. Oxford: Oxford University Press.

Popper, K (1959). *The logic of scientific discovery*. New York: Basic Books.

Pyke, S. & Agnew, N. (1991). *The science game*. Englewood Cliff, NJ: Prentice-Hall.

Quitkin, F. M., Stewart, J. W., McGrath, P. J., Nunes, E., Ocepek-Welikson, K., Tricamo, E., Rabkin, J. G., Ross, D., & Klein, D. F. (1993a). Loss of drug effects during continuation therapy. *American Journal of Psychiatry* 150:562–565.

Quitkin, F. M., Stewart, J. W., McGrath, P. J., Tricamo, E., Rabkin, J. G., Ocepek-Welikson, K., Nunes, E., Harrison, W., & Klein, D. F. (1993b). Columbia atypical depression. A subgroup of depressives with better response to MAOI than to tricyclic antidepressants or placebo. *British Journal of Psychiatry* Supplement 21:30–34.

Rabinowitz, F., Good, G., & Cozad, L. (1989). Rollo May: A Man of Myth and Meaning. *Journal of Counselling and Development* 67 (8): 436-442.

Ramirez, L. F. (1996). Ethnicity and psychopharmacology in Latin America. *Mt. Sinai Journal of Medicine* 63:330–331.

Randolph, F., Blasinsky, M., Leginski, W., Parker, L. B., & Goldman, H. H. (1997). Creating integrated service systems for homeless persons with mental illness: The ACCESS Program. Access to community care and effective services and supports. *Psychiatric Services* 48:369–373.

Rathas, S (1973). A 30 item schedule for assessing assertive behaviour. *Behavior Therapy* 4:398-406.

Reger, G.M. & Rogers, S.A. (2002). Diagnostic Differences in Religious Coping Among Individuals with Persistent Mental Illness. *Journal of Psychology and Christianity* 21 (4): 341-348.

Reznick, C. (2003). *Imagery for Kids*. Retrieved January 21, 2004, from Imagery for Kids Web Site: http://www.imageryforkids.com.

Richards, J. (1978). Early Indo-Aryan Social Structure. *Mankind Quarterly, 19*(2), 129-150. Robert Wood Johnson Foundation. (1990). Public attitudes toward people with chronic mental illnesses. Boston: Robert Wood Johnson Foundation Program on Chronic Mental Illnesses.

Robins, L. N., & Regier, D. A. (1991). *Psychiatric disorders in America: The Epidemiologic Catchment Area Study*. New York: Free Press.

Rogan, M. T., & LeDoux, J. E. (1996). Emotion: Systems, cells, synaptic plasticity. *Cell* 85:469–475.

Rorty, T. (1997). Is the truth out there?, *Times Higher Education Supplement* 6:June 1997.

Roy, W. (2001). *Making Societies*. Thousand Oaks, CA: Pine Forge Press.

Rubin, H. (1983). *Applied social research*. Columbus, OH: Charles E. Merril.

Rush, A. J., Stewart, R. S., Garver, D. L., & Waller, D. A. (1998). Neurobiological bases for psychiatric disorders. In R. N. Rosenberb & D. E. Pleasure (Eds.), *Comprehensive neurology* (2nd ed., pp. 555–603). New York: John Wiley and Sons.

Ryan, M. (1989). The American Parade IN: *The new cultural history*. Berkley: University of California Press.

Ryglewicz, H., & Glynn, L. (1993). Project change revisited: An experiment in entry or reentry into college. *Psychosocial Rehabilitation Journal* 17:69–81.

Sachs, G. S., Lafer, B., Stoll, A. L., Banov, M., Thibault, A. B., Tohen, M., & Rosenbaum, J. F. (1994). A double-blind trial of bupropion versus desipramine for bipolar depression. *Journal of Clinical Psychiatry* 55:391–393.

Sackeim, H. A. (1994). Continuation therapy following ECT: Directions for future research. *Psychopharmacology Bulletin* 30:501–521.

Samons, L. J. (2000). Socrates, Virtue and the Modern Professor. *Journal of Education* 182 (2): 19-28.

Sanders, N. K. (1987). *The Epic of Gilgamesh*. New York: Penguin.

Sartorius, T. C. (2003). Myth, meaning and mystery. *Arts and Activities* 132 (5): 32-36.

Sartre, J. P. (1956). *Being and Nothingness : Translation by Barnes, H..* New York: Philosophical Library.

Schultz, S. K., Miller, D. D., Oliver, S. E., Arndt, S., Flaum, M., & Andreasen, N. C. (1997). The life course of schizophrenia: Age and symptom dimensions. *Schizophrenia Research* 23:15–23.

Schutt, R. K., & Goldfinger, S. M. (1996). Housing preferences and perceptions of health and functioning among homeless mentally ill persons. *Psychiatric Services* 47:381–386.

Schwarzkopf, S. B., Nasrallah, H. A., Olson, S. C., Bogerts, B., McLaughlin, J. A., & Mitra, T. (1991). Family history and brain morphology in schizophrenia: An MRI study. *Psychiatry Research* 40:49–60.

Scott J. (1992). Chronic depression: Can cognitive therapy succeed when other treatments fail? *Behavioral Psychotherapy* 20:25–36.

Segal, G. (2000). Beyond Subjectivity: Spinoza's Cognitivism of the Emotions. *British Journal for the History of Philosophy* 8 (1): 1-19.

REFERENCES

Skinner, B. F. (1984). Behaviorism at fifty. In (Ed.), *Behavioral and Brain Sciences* (7 ed., pp. 615-667).

Smith, T., McCullough, M. & Poll, J. (2003). Religiousness and Depression: Evidence for a Main Effect and the Moderating Influence of Stressful Life Events. *Psychological Bulletin* 129 (4): 614-636.

Society for Existential Analysis. (2003). *Practitioners Contact List*. Retrieved February 6, 2003, from Society for Existential Analysis Web Site: http://www.existentialanalysis.co.uk/index.php?page=practioners

Solomon, R. C. (1972). *Phenomenology and Existentialism*. New York: Harper and Row.

Solomon, R. C. (1972). *Phenomenology and Existentialism*. New York: Harper & Row.

Spinelli, E. (1989). *The Interpreted World*. London: Sage.

Spinelli, E. (1994). *Demystifying psychotherapy*. London: Constable.

Spinelli, E. (n.d.). *Existential Psychotherapy – A Personal View*. Retrieved June 12, 2003, from http://www.alanmiles.net/old800/psychotherapy/psyexistential.htm.

Stein, M. (1987). Looking Backward: Archetypes in reconstruction. In Schwartz-Salant (Ed.), *Archetypal process in psychotherapy* (pp. 57-74). : .

Steinberg, D. (1998). The Method and Structure of Knowledge in Spinoza. *Pacific Philsophical Quarterly* 79 (2): 158-176.

Sturman, G. M. (1993). *The Career Discovery Project*. New York: Doubleday.

Sullivan, G. M., Coplan, J. D., & Gorman, J. M. (1998). Psychoneuroendocrinology of anxiety disorders. *Psychiatric Clinics of North America* 21:397–412.

Suppes, T., Baldessarini, R. J., Faedda, G. L., Tondo, L., & Tohen, M. (1993). Discontinuation of maintenance treatment in bipolar disorder: Risks and implications. *Harvard Review of Psychiatry* 1:131–144.

Susser, E., Hoek, H. W., & Brown, A. (1998). Neurodevelopmental disorders after prenatal famine: The story of the Dutch Famine Study. *American Journal of Epidemiology* 147:213–216.

Susser, E., Neugebauer, R., Hoek, H. W., Brown, A. S., Lin, S., Labovitz, D., & Gorman, J. M. (1996). Schizophrenia after prenatal famine. Further evidence. *Archives of General Psychiatry* 53:25–31.

Tamas, R. (2002). Is the modern Psyche undergoing a Rite of Passage? *ReVision* 24 (3): 2-9.

Tanzman, B. (1993). An overview of surveys of mental health consumers' preferences for housing and support services. *Hospital and Community Psychiatry* 44:450–455.

Taylor, M. (1995). Tuning In: An Interview with Emmy Van Deurzen-Smith. *Journal of Guidance and Counseling* 23 (1): .

Taylor, R. (1981). The Meaning of Life. In E. D. Klemke (Ed.), *The Meaning of Life* (1 ed., pp. 144-145). Oxford: Oxford University Press.

Teeter, E. (1997). *The Presentation of MAAT*. Chicago: Oriental Institute – University of Chicago.

Teiger, P. & Barron-Tieger, B. (1995) *Do What You ARE!* New York: Little Brown Company.

Tessler, R., & Gamache, G. (1994). Continuity of care, residence, and family burden in Ohio. *Milbank Quarterly* 72:149–170.

Thakker, J., & Ward, T. (1998). Culture and classification: The cross-cultural application of the DSM-IV. *Clinical Psychology Review* 18:501–529.

Thase, M. E. (1993). Maintenance treatments of recurrent affective disorders. *Current Opinions in Psychiatry* 6:16–21.

Thase, M. E. (1995). Reeducative psychotherapies. In G. O. Gabbard (Ed.), *Treatment of psychiatric disorders* (pp. 1169–1204). Washington, DC: American Psychiatric Press.

Ulbrich, P. M., Warheit, G. J., & Zimmerman, R. S. (1989). Race, socioeconomic status, and psychological distress: An examination of differential vulnerability. *Journal of Health and Social Behavior* 30:131–146.

Umbricht, D., & Kane, J. M. (1995). Risperidone: Efficacy and safety. Schizophrenia Bulletin 21:593–606.

U.S. Department of Education. (1998). Disability Forum Report–3. Housing and disability: Data needs, statistics and policy. Proceedings of the Third National Disability Statistics and Policy Forum. Washington, DC: National Institute on Disability and Rehabilitation Research.

U.S. Department of Health and Human Services. (1996). *Physical activity and health: A report of the Surgeon General.* Atlanta, GA: U.S. Department of Health and Human Services, Centers for Disease Control and Prevention, National Center for Chronic Disease Prevention and Health Promotion.

U.S. Department of Housing and Urban Development. (1994). *Worse case need for housing assistance in the U.S. in 1990 and 1991: A report to Congress.* Washington, DC: HUD Office of Policy Development and Research.

Vaillant, G. E. (1977). *Adaptation to life.* New York: Basic Books.

Van Deurzen, E. (2001). *Paradox and Passion in Psychotherapy.* New York: Wiley.

Van Os, J., & Marcelis, M. (1998). The ecogenetics of schizophrenia: A review. *Schizophrenia Research* 32:127–135.

Van Os, J., Wright, P., & Murray, R. M. (1997). Follow-up studies of schizophrenia. I: Natural history and non-psychopathological predictors of outcome. *European Psychiatry* 12:327S–341S.

Van Putten, T., Marder, S. R., & Mintz, J. (1990). A controlled dose comparison of haloperidol in newly admitted schizophrenic patients. *Archives of General Psychiatry* 47:754–758.

Van Tosh, L., & del Vecchio, P. (in press). *Consumer/survivor-operated self-help programs: A technical report.* Washington, DC: U.S. Department of Health and Human Services.

Vanelle, J. M. (1997). Refractory schizophrenia: Historical and currently prevailing criteria and definitions. *European Psychiatry* 12:321S–326S.

Van Neikerk, A. (1999). Death, Meaning and Tragedy. *South African Journal of Philosophy* 18 (4):408-426.

Wachtel, H. (1990). The second-messenger dysbalance hypothesis of affective disorders. *Pharmacopsychiatry* 23:27–32.

Wahl, O. F., Borostovik, L., & Rieppi, R. (1995). Schizophrenia in popular periodicals. *Community Mental Health Journal* 31:239–248.

Wamble, M. (2002). St Augustine's Confessions. *U.S. Catholic* 67:17.

Weinberger, D. R. (1995). Schizophrenia as a neurodevelopmental disorder. In S. R. Hirsch & D. R. Weinberger (Eds.), *Schizophrenia* (pp. 293–323). Oxford, England, Cambridge, MA: Blackwell Science Ltd.

Weinberger, D. R., & Lipska, B. K. (1995). Cortical maldevelopment, antipsychotic drugs, and schizophrenia: A search for common ground. *Schizophrenia Research* 16:87–110.

Weiner, R. D., & Krystal, A. D. (1994). The present use of electroconvulsive therapy. *Annual Review of Medicine* 45:273–281.

Weiss, J. M. (1991). Stress-induced depression: Critical neurochemical and electrophysiological changes. In J. Madden (Ed.), *Neurobiology of learning, emotion, and affect* (pp. 123–154). New York: Raven Press.

Weiss, E. L., Longhurst, J. G., & Mazure, C. M. (1999). Childhood sexual abuse as a risk factor for depression in women: Psychosocial and neurobiological correlates. *American Journal of Psychiatry* 156:816–828.

Weissman, M. M., Bland, R. C., Canino, G. J., Faravelli, C., Greenwald, S., Hwu, H. G., Joyce, P. R., Karam, E. G., Lee, C. K., Lellouch, J., Lepine, J. P., Newman, S. C., Oakley-Browne, M. A., Rubio-Stipec, M., Wells, J. E. Wickramaratne, P. J., Wittchen, H. U., & Yeh, E. K. (1997). The cross-national epidemiology of panic disorder. *Archives of General Psychiatry* 54:305–309.

Wilkinson, P. (2000). *A terrible beauty: a history of people and ideas that shaped the modern world.* London: Weidenfeld & Nicholson.

Williams, A. (1994). Clinical sociometry to define space in family systems. *Journal of Group Psychotherapy, Psychodrama and Sociometry* 47 (3):126-144.

Williams, J.T. (1995). *Pooh and the philosophers.* London: Methuen.

Wood , L. (2003). Living by the Word. *Christian Century, 120*(10), 20-22. World Health Organization. (1997). Psychosocial rehabilitation: A consensus statement. *International Journal of Mental Health* 26:77–85.

Wyatt, R. J., Green, M. F., & Tuma, A. H. (1997). Long-term morbidity associated with delayed treatment of first admission schizophrenic patients: A re-analysis of the Camarillo State Hospital data. *Psychological Medicine* 27:261–268.

Yardley, T. & Honess, T. (1987). *Self and Identity: Psychosocial perspectives.* Chichester: John Wiley.

Yehuda, R. (1999). Biological factors associated with susceptibility to post-traumatic stress disorder. *Canadian Journal of Psychiatry* 44:34–39.

Yolken, R. H., & Torrey, E. F. (1995). Viruses, schizophrenia, and bipolar disorder. *Clinical Microbiology Reviews* 8:131–145.

Yuen, O., Caligiuri, M. P., Williams, R., & Dickson, R. A. (1996). Tardive dyskinesia and positive and negative symptoms of schizophrenia. A study using instrumental measures. *British Journal of Psychiatry* 168:702–708.

Zaharia, M. D., Kulczycki, J., Shanks, N., Meaney, M. J., & Anisman, H. (1996). The effects of early postnatal stimulation on Morris water-maze acquisition in adult mice: Genetic and maternal factors. *Psychopharmacology* 128:227–239.

Zalewski, C., Johnson-Selfridge, M. T., Ohriner, S., Zarrella, K., & Seltzer, J. C. (1998). A review of neuropsychological differences between paranoid and nonparanoid schizophrenia patients. *Schizophrenia Bulletin* 24:127–145.

Zuroff, D. (1982). Person, situation and person by situation interaction components in person perception. *Journal of Personality* 50 (1): 1-14.

INDEX OF PEOPLE

Adam, 19
Ahenakew, K., 65-68
Anselm (Saint), 42
Aquinas, Thomas, 92-95
Baenson, I., 39
Bonhoeffer, D., 49, 52, 98
Brunner, E., 92
Calvin, John, 15, 27
Darwin, Charles, 14
Descartes, 35
Eggose, L., 83
Enkidu, 29
Eve, 19
Euclid, 77
Frankl, Viktor, 23
Freud, Sigmund, 81-82
Gilgamesh, 29-30
Gorres, ix
Heidegger, M., 23
Hegel, M., ix
Husserl, E., 9
Jesus, 44 * 47, 87, 91-98
Jung, C., 21, 29
Kant, I., 16
Kierkegaard, Soren, 17, 26, 32
Luther, Martin, 15, 27, 51
Lone Man, 18
Meno, 35
Merleau Ponty, Maurice, 9, 56
Newton, Isaac, 77
Nietzche, Frederick, preface
Paul (Saint), 34, 38
Plato, 36
Pontius Pilate, 52
Rajaratnam, K., 55-58
Rank, O., ix

Rotterdam, Erasmus of, * 15, 59-60
Sartre, 9
Schelling, ix
Schleiermacher, ix
Shiva-Krishna, C., 75-80
Siduru, 29-30
Siegel, C., 99
Soggie, H., 2
Spinelli, E., 69-73.
Titus, S., 61-64.
Tysdal, B., x, 1-11,
Van Deurzen, 23

INDEX OF TOPICS

Aboriginals, 18, 25, 65-68
absolute, 67-68, 75-80
Ad Fontis, 15
Anteyokanuk, 25
autobiography, 49-52
autopoeics, 3-11, 20, 24-25, 39, 89
bodily essence, 3-4, 7, 9-10, 36
bodily knowing, 35-39
boundary, 4, 6-7
brain stem, 3-11, 39, 79
buffalo, 18
Catholic, 52, 61-64
cells, 3-10, 30
cellular identity, 5-9, 14
cellular thinking, 5-9
cerebellum, 7-9, 39
Christian worldview, ix, x, 51, 55-58, 61-64, 83-84 91-99
Christmas fireplace, 8
Cree, 25, 66-67
DALIT, 55
death, 11, 13, 17, 20-25, 29-37, 46-47, 55-56, 70-72, 79, 94-99
DNA, 4
economics, 55-58
empiricism, x
enzymes, 14
Existential
 meaning of work, 23-27, 95-98
 source, 30
 work, 30
 void, vii
Existo, 1, 89
Fall, The, 20, 93
family of origin, 20, 50
frontal lobe, 8, 89

font, 13-21, 24-26, 37, 40
Fons, 1, 11, 13-21, 24-26, 39, 41, 89, 91-99
Fons Vitae, 14-21, 89, 94-98
God, 17, 21, 27, 30, 32-38, 44-48, 51-52, 55, 59, 61-64, 70-71, 79, 87 91-98
Greeks (Classical), 10, 26
guided imagery, 43-48
guru, 75
idiocy, 59- 60
ignorance, 17, 56-58, 81-82, 98
Image Bearer, 91-98
intuition, x
left temporal lobe, 4-11, 89
leprosy, 83-84
Logotherapy, 23
Lone Man, 18
Manitou, 25, 66-68
Mark (Gospel of), 27
matter, 75-78
mythic, 13, 15-17, 24, 26, 33, 40
mythopoeics, 6-18, 43, 50-51, 89
Mortalitas, 1, 11, 24-25, 29-33, 39-41, 90-92
Nazism, 25
NeoDarwinism, 13-15
Nobel Conference, 19
Noumena, 16, 37, 90
occipital lobe, 7, 39
Opus, 11, 19, 23-27, 33, 39-41, 90, 94-97
Opus Vitae, 23-27, 90
Origin of the Species, 14
parietal lobe, 8
personal meaning, vii, xi, 3-11, 13

personality type, 23, 95
phenomenon, 16
Powecan, 25
pre-frontal lobe, 8
priesthood (of all believers), 27
religion, 13, 16-20, 39-42, 51, 63, 72, 81, 93
right temporal lobe, 8-9
RNA, 14
Roman Catholic, 61- 64
terrorist (terrorism), 55-58, 85-87
thalamus, 7-8
therapy, 69-73

About the Author

Neil Soggie was raised in Saskatchewan, Canada. He is currently a professor of Psychology at Atlantic Baptist University in Moncton, New Brunswick, Canada. He is an advocate for life long learning and global issues as well as a student of the great existential phenomenological psychotherapist Ernesto Spinelli. Dr. Soggie holds doctoral degrees from the United States, South Africa and England.

Other Contributors

Brian Tysdal was raised in Saskatchewan, Canada. Formerly a recording artist, Professor Tysdal is currently a popular lecturer in the areas of *Weltanschauung and the philosophy of constructed reality*. Professor Tysdal specializes in the integration of reality constructs and is an outspoken opponent of Platonic idealism.

Heidi Soggie was raised in British Columbia, Canada. A specialist in Leadership and Human Services she has distinguished herself in service to both youth and the elderly. As the Director of Student Development (and former director of the Youth Leadership program) at Atlantic Baptist University, she continues to challenge people to live authentic lives. Heidi Soggie is a popular lecturer and researcher in the areas of existential and religious well-being.

www.ingramcontent.com/pod-product-compliance
Lightning Source LLC
Chambersburg PA
CBHW021409290426
44108CB00010B/450